Welcome

TRY JAMIE MAGAZINE NOW! See page 164 to have

Jamie drop through your letterbox every two months

JAMIE'S FAVOURITE

You hold in your hands a collection of our favourite recipes from 2010. As always, my thanks go to all our wonderful contributors for the delicious recipes they've created and the photographers who've helped bring them to life. All recipes have been carefully tested in the Jamie kitchens, so you know you can rely on them whether you're in a mad dash to prepare a midweek family meal or want something special for a weekend brunch. We've signposted some of our favourites with tags such as 'Jamie's Favourite', 'Cheap & Easy', 'Fast Food' to help you decide what to cook. These are some of our favourites; why not send us one of yours? Email it to contact@jamiemagazine.com and we might publish the best!

andyhams

Editor

Back by popular demand, it's our second yearbook! And what a year we're reviewing. Pulling our favourite recipes from the past seven issues for this yearbook has been a joy, but also a struggle because we've been spoilt for choice. But I think we've chosen well, and I hope the beautiful recipes in this chunky mag serve you well for years to come. Of course they embrace all seasons, and as much great produce as we could squeeze in. But on top of that, they'll cover you for any occasion, on any day of the week, at any budget and across all cooking levels.

If you're new to *Jamie Magazine*, this yearbook should give you a sense of the brilliant recipes, places and people we like to shout about. As a magazine, we're evolving with each new issue, and having a great time in the process. I hope that comes across as you cook the recipes in here, whether they're mine, Andy's, or written by one of the great chefs or other wonderful contributors who've worked with us. Here's to another year of incredible food.

James

Editor at Large

106

148

124

54

6

90

ALL RECIPES
TESTED IN THE
JAMIE
OLIVER
KITCHENS

36

70

156

Contents

Breakfasts, snacks & starters

Launch yourself into the day with a substantial breakfast inspired by global flavours, whether it's Spanish-style eggs (page 7) or Aussie avocado on toast (page 11). Perk up your day (or someone else's) with chilli sausage rolls (page 20) or pane cunzato (page 17) and wow dinner guests with handmade Vietnamese summer rolls (page 14)

GYPSY-STYLE BAKED EGGS

TOASTED GRANOLA
WITH CHEWY FRUIT

GYPSY-STYLE BAKED EGGS

Recipe from Nathan Sasi

This Spanish-accented dish makes a lovely brunch, or shared starter, as it is served at Alira restaurant in Sydney.

Serves 1 for brunch

- 1 mild chorizo, cut into 1cm slices
- A small handful of cooked peas
- 2 eggs
- Grilled sourdough, to serve

Roasted tomato sauce

- 500g tomatoes, quartered
- ½ carrot, chopped
- ¼ leek, cut into 4
- ½ red onion, chopped
- 3 garlic cloves, roughly chopped
- 4 parsley stalks
- 2 sprigs of rosemary
- 1 bay leaf
- 1 tsp chilli powder
- 1 tbsp smoked paprika
- 100ml white wine
- 30ml sherry vinegar

1 For the roasted tomato sauce, place all the ingredients apart from the wine and the vinegar on a tray and roast at 200C/gas 6 for 25 minutes, or until the vegetables and tomato have coloured. Once everything is cooked, place a pan on high heat and add the wine and vinegar. When reduced by half, add the vegetables and cook for a further minute or so, till well combined and thick. Place the sauce in a blender and blend until smooth. Season well.
2 Using a griddle pan, cook the chorizo slices for 1 minute on each side. Pour a good layer of sauce into a small ovenproof dish. Add the chorizo and peas and crack in the eggs. Bake in the oven at 200C/gas 6 for 12 minutes, or until the whites are cooked but the yolks are still runny. Serve with grilled sourdough to dip into the yolks.

....

TOASTED GRANOLA WITH CHEWY FRUIT

Don't be afraid to toast the oats until really golden as this gives the granola a more caramelised flavour.

Makes about 700g

- 8 tbsp honey
- 300g rolled oats
- 40g each of sunflower and pumpkin seeds
- 75g skin-on almonds, chopped
- 30g desiccated coconut
- 50g dried sour cherries
- 50g each of dates, dried apricots and peaches, chopped

1 Preheat the oven to 150C/gas 2. Warm through the honey in a pan. Spread out the oats, seeds, nuts and coconut on a large baking tray, pour over the warm honey, then mix everything together with and pop the tray in the oven for 20 minutes, stirring every so often.
2 When the 20 minutes is up, add all the fruit, stir once (and try not to touch again until it is cool) and put it back in the oven for another 10 minutes. It should be clumping together nicely.
3 Remove from the oven and allow to cool before breaking it up and storing in jars or airtight containers for up to 1 month. Lovely with yoghurt and fresh or poached seasonal fruit.

COCONUT BREAD

CORNBREAD FRENCH TOAST, HALLOUMI & CHILLI JAM

This is great as a breakfast, brunch or light supper. Leftover cornbread will keep for a week wrapped in greaseproof paper.

Serves 4

- 200g cornmeal or polenta
- 100g self-raising flour
- 2 tsp baking powder
- 2 handfuls of sweetcorn kernels
- 4 eggs, beaten
- 300ml milk
- 320ml yoghurt
- 75g unsalted butter, melted
- 50g cheddar cheese, grated
- 1 red chilli, finely chopped
- A knob of butter
- 200g halloumi, cut into 8 slices

Chilli jam

- Olive oil
- 2 red onions, finely sliced
- 2 garlic cloves, sliced
- 8 red chillies, deseeded and sliced
- 400g cherry tomatoes, halved
- 4 tbsp dark brown sugar
- Juice of 4 limes

1 Preheat the oven to 190C/gas 5 and butter a 20-22cm square tin. Put the dry ingredients in a bowl with the corn kernels and mix. Combine half the beaten egg with the milk and yoghurt and stir through the dry ingredients. Add the melted butter and stir to combine. Pour into the tin and bake for 30-40 minutes, or until a skewer inserted into the centre comes out clean. After 20 minutes, sprinkle over the cheddar and chilli and return to the oven. When cooked, allow to cool for 5 minutes, then turn out onto a rack.
2 For the chilli jam, heat a saucepan and add a drizzle of oil. Fry the onions and garlic for 10 minutes. Add the chillies, tomatoes, sugar and lime juice and simmer down to a sticky sauce.
3 Dip eight 2cm-slices of cornbread into the rest of the beaten egg. In a pan, heat the butter and fry the bread on each side until golden and crusty. Remove from the pan and keep warm.
4 Quickly fry the halloumi until golden on each side. Place a slice on each piece of cornbread and spoon over some chilli jam. Serve with baby leaves and herbs.

COCONUT BREAD

If you have the time to make it, this is an easy loaf to bake in the morning for a late breakfast. Toast any leftover slices, or use to make a tropical trifle.

Serves 8

- 3 eggs
- 400ml milk
- 300g self-raising flour
- 200g caster sugar
- 200g desiccated coconut
- 1 vanilla pod, split, seeds scraped
- 100g unsalted butter, melted
- Lime marmalade, to serve

1 Preheat the oven to 180C/gas 4 and butter a 22cm x 8cm loaf tin. Whisk together the eggs and milk. Put the flour, sugar, coconut and vanilla seeds in a bowl and make a well in the centre. Gradually stir in the egg mixture, then the butter, and mix until smooth.
2 Pour the mixture into the loaf tin and bake for about 1 hour, or until a metal skewer inserted in the centre comes out clean. Allow your loaf to cool in the tin for a few minutes, then turn it out onto a wire rack. Slice and serve with a good spreading of lime marmalade (or whichever conserve you fancy).

VEGETARIAN

CORNBREAD FRENCH TOAST, HALLOUMI & CHILLI JAM

E for B

Eggs are the ultimate breakfast ingredient. If you like yours scrambled, punch up the flavour by stirring through snipped chives, strips of smoked salmon, or some chopped tomatoes. A frittata is a versatile way to use leftovers. Gently fry bacon with some sliced roast potato, then pour over beaten eggs. Stir the eggs gently, then cook till set, finishing under the grill to firm up the top. Grated courgette, mixed with chopped parsley and a handful of crumbled feta, makes a great frittata filling, likewise sliced mushrooms fried with prosciutto and thyme leaves, or roast squash and slices of red pepper. For a spicier start to the day, drizzle oil into a hot pan, crack in your eggs, and sprinkle with crushed cumin seeds, chilli flakes, salt and pepper and lemon juice. Put in a hot oven until cooked to your liking, then served scattered with ripped mint leaves.

HUEVOS RANCHEROS

AVOCADO & ROASTED TOMATOES ON TOAST

This is the kind of breakfast that you find in cafés across Australia. You can't beat the way the creamy, nutty avocado combines with the tangy cheese and sweet tomato.

Serves 4

- 4 plum or 12 cherry tomatoes, halved
- Olive oil
- A bunch of basil, leaves picked
- 1 lemon, halved
- 3 ripe avocados
- 4 slices of sourdough bread
- 150g feta cheese
- 4 handfuls of rocket

1 You can do this part the night before. Preheat the oven to 150C/gas 2. Place the tomatoes cut-side up on a baking tray, season and drizzle with olive oil. Roast slowly for 1½–2 hours, or until they are sticky and dried out.
2 When you're ready for breakfast, pound the basil in a mortar with a pinch of salt until you have a paste. Pour in a good splash of olive oil and squeeze in the juice of ½ lemon. Halve your avocados and scoop out the flesh. Place in a bowl, squeeze in the other lemon half and season. Gently mash with a fork to bring it all together.
3 Toast the bread, then divide between 4 plates, spread on the mashed avocado and top with the tomatoes. Top each with crumbled feta, a handful of rocket and a drizzle of basil oil.

HUEVOS RANCHEROS

This is a Mexican-inspired way of cooking your eggs that'll give you a bit of spice and heat to kick off your day.

Serves 2

- 1 onion, diced
- 2 garlic cloves, sliced
- 1–2 green chillies, chopped
- Olive oil
- 1 x 400g tin chopped tomatoes
- 1–2 tsp ground cumin
- A small bunch of coriander, chopped
- 4 corn tortillas
- 2–4 eggs
- 1 lime, plus extra to serve
- 1 red chilli, finely sliced, to serve

1 Preheat the oven to 150C/gas 2. In a large frying pan over medium heat, sweat the onion, garlic and green chillies in olive oil until softened. Add the tomatoes, cumin, half the coriander and season. Turn down the heat and simmer for 10-15 minutes, until reduced.
2 Meanwhile, wrap the tortillas in tin foil and place them in the oven. In a second frying pan, fry 1-2 eggs per person. Add a squeeze of lime to the salsa and take it off the heat. Place 2 tortillas on each plate, then top with some salsa and the eggs. Scatter with the remaining coriander and the sliced red chilli and serve with lime wedges.

MAKE AHEAD

POACHED DRIED FRUIT

Make this the day before and serve cold from the fridge or slightly warmed.

Serves 2

- 750ml darjeeling tea
- 500g golden caster sugar
- 1.5kg mixed dried fruits (apricots, prunes, figs, apple, sour cherries)
- Grated zest of 1 orange
- 1 cinnamon stick
- 1 vanilla pod
- 1 star anise
- Greek-style yoghurt, or muesli, to serve

1 Combine the tea and sugar in a pan and simmer over a low heat to make a syrup. Add the remaining ingredients, turn the heat right down and gently poach the fruit for about 45 minutes, until it has absorbed the tea flavours. Allow to cool, then chill overnight in the fridge. Serve with thick, plain Greek-style yoghurt or muesli.

BROWN SEED & FRUIT BREAD

Makes 1 small loaf

- 350g wholemeal bread flour
- 200g plain flour
- 75g oatbran or wheatbran, or a mixture
- 1 tbsp baking powder
- 80g mixed seeds (such as linseeds, poppy seeds, sesame seeds, pumpkin seeds, sunflower seeds, hemp seeds)
- 125g dried fruit (sultanas, figs or apricots, or a mixture of all three)
- About 650ml milk

1 Preheat the oven to 180C/gas 4. Mix the dry ingredients together in a bowl and add just enough milk to form a moist dough – about 650ml.
2 Grease a 20cm x 8cm loaf tin and spoon in the dough. Smooth out the top and bake for about an hour or until the bread is golden brown and sounds hollow when its base is tapped. Set aside to cool, then serve with butter for breakfast and with strong cheese and chutney for supper.

BROWN SEED & FRUIT BREAD

Feeling fruity

Both recipes on this page highlight the versatility of dried apricots – and it doesn't stop there. For a real North African flavour, try adding chopped dried apricots to cooked couscous, along with pistachios and parsley, or throwing whole ones into a lamb tagine. Combine chopped dried apricots with hazelnuts, sage, onion and breadcrumbs in a stuffing for poultry. Add a handful of chopped apricots next time you make flapjacks or stir into porridge. Simmer whole in orange juice and honey, then have over ice cream. Split them, then stuff with mascarpone, or fill with ricotta and pop under a hot grill for 3 minutes. And, if you're facing a long car journey with children, make sure you pack some dried apricots to offer instead of sweets.

POSH SOLDIERS

SUMMER ROLLS

POSH SOLDIERS
Enough for 8 soldiers

- 2 large, long green banana chillies
- Extra-virgin olive oil
- Red wine vinegar
- 150g fresh crabmeat
- A small bunch of dill, fronds chopped
- Juice of 1 lemon
- 1 tbsp mayonnaise
- A pinch of smoked paprika (optional)
- 2 big slices of sourdough, toasted
- 1 garlic clove, halved
- 4–5 cherry tomatoes, quartered

1 Under a hot grill or in a griddle pan, grill the chillies until their skins are charred. Put in a bowl and cover with clingfilm to steam off the skins. Once cool, remove the seeds and skin. Finely slice, season, add a little oil and a swig of vinegar.
2 In a bowl, dress the crab with the dill, lemon juice, equal amounts of oil, mayo and paprika. Taste and season if needed.
3 Rub the bread with the garlic. Drizzle with oil, slice into soldiers and divide the chilli between the toasts, top with the crab, and scatter over the tomatoes.

SUMMER ROLLS
Once you get the hang of it, this classic Vietnamese snack is easy to make. It's delicious with shredded pork or chicken or with loads of crunchy julienned veg, such as carrot, cabbage and mushrooms.
Serves 4

- 12 rice paper wrappers/sheets
- 200g prawns, cooked and peeled
- 50g rice vermicelli, cooked
- 1 bunch each of mint, coriander and thai basil, leaves picked
- ½ cucumber, julienned
- 4 spring onions, sliced

Dipping sauce
- 1 red chilli, finely sliced
- 2 tbsp each soy sauce and fish sauce
- Juice of 1 lime

1 Making one roll at a time, soften a rice paper wrapper in hot water, then lay on a damp cloth. Place the prawns a third of the way down. Top with the remaining ingredients and roll up, tucking in the sides as you go. Mix the sauce ingredients, diluting with water, to taste. Place the sauce in dipping bowls and serve with the summer rolls.

BROAD BEAN & WILD FENNEL BRUSCHETTA
Recipe by Gennaro Contaldo
Wild fennel grows in fields and roadsides throughout England during the summer. It lacks the bulb of its cultivated relative. Instead the juicy stalks and frond-like leaves are used. As with all wild food, use field notes to ensure correct identification.
Serves 4

- 4 tbsp extra-virgin olive oil
- 200g bacon, sliced
- 2 onions, finely chopped
- 500g podded baby broad beans
- 100ml vegetable stock
- A handful of wild fennel or regular fennel tops, chopped
- 4 slices of toasted ciabatta

1 Heat the olive oil in a frying pan on a medium heat. Add the bacon and onions and fry until softened. Stir in the broad beans and cook for 1 minute. Add the stock, then season well with sea salt and black pepper. Reduce the heat and simmer until the beans are tender, but hold their shape and the stock has been absorbed. Take the pan off the heat, stir in the fennel and serve on the ciabatta with a drizzle of olive oil.

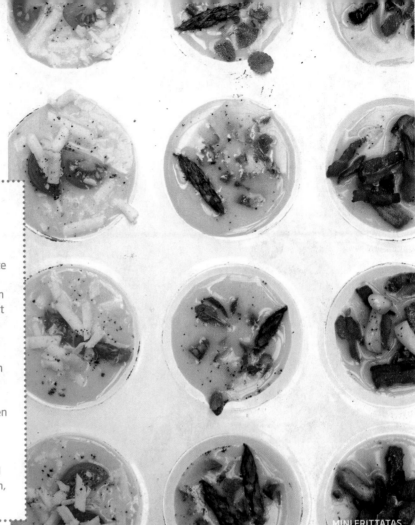
MINI FRITTATAS

Fold & flip

Omelettes are a great way of using up leftovers. To make a basic omelette, use 2–3 eggs per person and a 15cm omelette pan. Break the eggs into a bowl, season and whisk with a fork. Heat the pan, then add a knob of butter. Pour in the eggs, tilt until evenly distributed and wait 5 seconds. Using a spoon, pull the cooked edges of the omelette to the centre and tip the pan to cook any runny egg. Fold in half and transfer to a plate. You can vary this recipe by adding finely chopped chervil, tarragon and chives to the beaten egg for an omelette fines herbes. Or try frying a little pancetta and mushrooms before adding the egg, or top your omelette with spinach leaves or smoked mackerel. Cheese is another top addition, from cheddar to soft goat's cheese.

PANE CUNZATO

This dish has made the small café Da Alfredo, in Sicily, famous. It takes the classic combination of tomatoes, bread and olive oil and throws in ingredients such as aubergine, cheese, seafood and capers. Perfect for a snack, or light lunch or dinner.
Serves 2–4

- 1 round loaf of Italian-style crusty bread
- 4 tbsp extra-virgin olive oil, plus extra for rubbing and drizzling
- 1 tsp dried oregano
- 4 tbsp stoned, crushed green olives
- 10 ripe cherry tomatoes, halved
- 1 red onion, thinly sliced
- 12 marinated anchovy fillets
- 2 tbsp capers, rinsed and drained
- 4 tbsp chopped fresh basil, plus leaves from 2 sprigs of basil
- 1 tsp dried chilli flakes or finely chopped fresh chilli

1 Halve the bread, rub the cut sides with a little olive oil and sprinkle with dried oregano. Transfer to your plates.
2 Place olives, tomatoes and onions in a small bowl. Add olive oil, season generously with sea salt and freshly ground black pepper and combine well.
3 Place the tomato mix on the bread halves. Add the anchovies, capers and chopped basil. Sprinkle with the fresh chilli or flakes, drizzle with extra-virgin olive oil and garnish with basil leaves.

MINI FRITTATAS
Makes 12

- 6 eggs
- 2 tbsp milk
- Fillings: grilled asparagus and fresh mint; fried mushrooms and bacon; or grated cheese and cherry tomatoes

1 In a jug, beat together the eggs and milk and season generously. Grease a 12-hole tart or cupcake tin and divide the egg mixture equally between the holes and add your preferred filling. Bake at 180C/gas 4, for 12–15 minutes, until crisp and golden. Leave to cool a little before removing from the tray and serve immediately as brunch or a light lunch, perhaps with a simple salad.

OYSTER PO'BOY

Sarnies & shells

The po' boy (left) is an institution from the American Deep South, and there are many versions. Instead of oysters, try battering and deep-frying big raw prawns, soft-shell crab or pieces of white fish. Vegetarians might like pieces of courgette, aubergine or mushroom. Or spread the baguette with mustard and mayo, pile high with french fries, pickles, chillies, red onion and herbs. Also popular in New Orleans, 'rockefeller' (right) is a classic way of cooking oysters. Try them 'kilpatrick' – topped with fried bacon, breadcrumbs, and a splash of worcestershire sauce, then grilled for 5-10 minutes. At Cafe di Stasio in Melbourne, they bake oysters in a hot oven after topping them with a mixture of butter, grated parmesan and grated horseradish.

OYSTERS ROCKEFELLER

OYSTER PO' BOY

A po' boy is a classic New Orleans sandwich of deep-fried oysters in a crusty baguette. The name is a shortened version of 'poor boy', as it was a cheap way of filling your stomach. This version encases the soft oysters in tempura batter, which goes really crisp for a textural contrast.

Makes 4

- Vegetable oil, for deep-frying
- 20 oysters, shucked
- Paprika, for sprinkling
- 4 small baguette or ciabatta rolls
- Cos, little gem and/or wild rocket leaves
- 8 cherry tomatoes
- ½ cucumber, peeled into strips

Tempura batter
- 2 egg yolks
- 350ml iced water
- 1 tsp cornflour
- 175g self-raising flour

Tartare sauce
- 150g good-quality mayonnaise
- 1 tsp capers, finely chopped
- Zest and juice of 1 lemon
- 2 cornichons, finely chopped
- A few sprigs of flat-leaf parsley, roughly chopped

1 To make the tartare sauce, mix all the ingredients in a bowl. Line up everything else before you begin frying the oysters.
2 In a large, deep saucepan, heat the vegetable oil to 180C. If you don't have a thermometer, carefully drop in a small cube of bread; it should sizzle gently and turn golden-brown in 30 seconds.
3 Meanwhile, for the batter, whisk the yolks into the iced water, then stir in the flours – don't whisk until it's smooth, you want a few lumps. Add the oysters to coat, then gently shake off the excess. In batches, carefully lower them into the hot oil and cook until golden brown and crisp on all sides. Remove with a slotted spoon, drain on kitchen paper, then sprinkle with paprika and sea salt.
4 To assemble your po' boys, slice open the bread rolls, spoon some tartare sauce on the bottom, then add the salad leaves, tomatoes and cucumber. Top with the hot fried oysters, and spoon on a little more tartare sauce, then finish with a squeeze of lemon. This is best enjoyed with a pint of Guinness.

OYSTERS ROCKEFELLER

Serves 2 as an entrée

- 6 oysters in deep shells, shucked, with the shells retained
- 500g rock salt, to sit the oysters on
- 3 spring onions, topped, tailed and roughly chopped
- 1 celery stick, roughly chopped
- A few sprigs of tarragon
- A small handful of stale breadcrumbs
- A few drops of Tabasco
- 1 tbsp butter, softened

1 Lay an oyster on the deeper half of each of the shells, then place the shells on a bed of rock salt in a small baking tray.
2 Using a hand-held blender or a food processor, blitz the remaining ingredients to a chunky paste. Season carefully with black pepper and a little salt, then spoon a little on top of each oyster. Cook under a hot grill for about 10 minutes, until crisp and golden-brown.

HOMEMADE LIME PICKLE

CHILLI SAUSAGE ROLLS

Serves 6-8 as a snack

- 3-4 red chillies, to taste
- 500g pork sausage meat
- ½ tsp smoked paprika
- 500g puff pastry
- 2 egg yolks, beaten with a splash of milk
- 1 tbsp cumin seeds

1 Preheat the oven to 180C/gas 4. Pierce the chillies, then toast over a gas flame or a hot grill until black and blistered. Place in a bowl, cover with clingfilm and leave to cool. When cool enough to handle, pull off and discard the skins, then scoop out the seeds - or leave them in if you want fireworks! Chop the chilli flesh and mix with the sausage, paprika and a pinch of pepper.
2 Sprinkle a work surface with flour. Cut the pastry in half and roll out into 2 strips, 50cm x 15cm each. Shape the sausage meat into 2 sausage shapes and place along the middle of each strip. Coat the pastry either side of the sausage with the egg mixture. Fold the pastry over and press down to seal. Brush the tops of the sausage rolls with egg wash, sprinkle with cumin seeds and sea salt. Cut into 5cm lengths and place on a non-stick baking sheet. Bake for 20 minutes, until risen, puffed up and an irresistible golden brown.

HOMEMADE LIME PICKLE

Makes 320g

Usually served as an accompaniment to curries, lime pickle makes a great pre-dinner snack served with poppadoms or crisps.

- 250g preserved lemons, drained
- Vegetable oil
- 1 tbsp black mustard seeds
- 1 tbsp grated ginger
- 2 green chillies, chopped
- 75g hot curry paste
- 1 tbsp tomato purée
- Zest and juice of 2 limes
- A few sprigs of coriander, chopped
- 8 shop-bought poppadoms, to serve

1 Halve and deseed the preserved lemons. Chop finely and set aside.
2 Heat a saucepan over a medium heat, and add a splash of oil. Add the mustard seeds and when they pop, add the ginger, chillies, curry paste and tomato purée. Stir, and fry for a moment to combine, before adding the preserved lemon, lime zest and juice and coriander. Season generously, cook for a minute, transfer to a bowl and allow to cool before serving with poppadoms.

CROWD
PLEASER

TOMATO & COURGETTE TART

QUAIL EGGS & CELERY SALT HOLLANDAISE

TOMATO & COURGETTE TART

Serves 4-6

- 300g puff pastry
- 2 eggs and 1 egg yolk, beaten
- 200g ricotta
- Zest of 1 lemon
- A small bunch of thyme
- 350g cherry tomatoes, halved
- 1 courgette, sliced with a peeler
- Olive oil

1 Preheat oven to 180C/gas 4. Roll out the pastry to a rectangle that's about 35cm x 20cm. Score a border 2cm from the edge and prick the middle with a fork.
2 Mix most of the eggs with the ricotta, lemon zest, thyme and season. Spread over the inner rectangle. Top with the tomatoes, courgette and a little oil. Brush the border with the remaining beaten egg and bake for 20 minutes, until filling is set and pastry is golden.

QUAIL EGGS & CELERY SALT HOLLANDAISE

Serves 4

- 400ml vegetable oil
- 2 tsp celery salt
- 1 tbsp sour cream
- 3 tbsp good-quality hollandaise sauce
- 12 quail eggs
- 3 tbsp flour
- 1 egg, beaten
- 50g breadcrumbs
- Chopped chives, to serve

1 Heat the oil in a deep-frying pan. Mix the celery salt, sour cream and hollandaise. Boil the eggs for 2½ minutes, then plunge them into cold water and peel. Coat in the flour, then beaten egg, then breadcrumbs. When the oil is at 180C (use a thermometer or carefully drop in a small cube of bread; it should sizzle gently, rise and turn golden-brown in 30 seconds), very carefully add the eggs and cook in batches for 1 minute, until golden and crisp. Serve with the flavoured hollandaise sauce and chives.

HUMMUS 3 WAYS

Serves 4

- 1 tin chickpeas, drained
- 1 tbsp tahini
- 2 garlic cloves
- Juice of 1 lemon
- 3 tbsp olive oil
- 1 tsp harissa (optional)
- 3-4 roasted red peppers (optional)
- Toasted pita and sliced raw vegetables, to serve

1 In a blender, whizz up the chickpeas, tahini, garlic, lemon juice and olive oil. Season generously and add more olive oil if necessary until the mixture is smooth; taste again, and add more seasoning or lemon juice if desired. You can either leave the hummus plain, or add the harissa or red peppers and blitz once more. Serve with halved and toasted pita bread slices and crunchy crudités, or in sandwiches.

FAST
FOOD

The bartender's best friend

There is nothing quite like the perfect gin and tonic. The tinkling of ice cubes, the bite of the tonic, the citrus zing of the lime... You'll want to make sure you don't spoil it by using any old gin.

Thankfully you don't have to as Tanqueray® London Dry Gin has a rich, multilayered flavour that comes from specially selected ingredients sourced all over the world. Gin was at the height of its popularity when Charles Tanqueray decided to make the finest example possible at his Bloomsbury distillery. The result was a sublimely balanced gin made from a complex combination of refreshing juniper berries, peppery coriander and aromatic angelica, which gives it a unique taste that sets it apart from the rest.

Tanqueray is widely regarded as the bartender's choice of gin, though you don't have to be a mixologist to enjoy it – the Blackcurrant Bramble cocktail (left) is easy to make at home. Just pour 35ml of Tanqueray gin over ice before stirring in 25ml lemon juice and 12.5ml crème de cassis. Finally, stir in 1 tsp brown sugar and, once dissolved, garnish with a curl of lemon rind and a plump blackberry (units: 1.8).

If you'd prefer something even simpler, why not try the classic Tanqueray & Tonic (far left)? To make, simply squeeze the juice of a lime wedge into a tapered highball glass, then fill the glass two-thirds full of ice. Pour in 35ml of Tanqueray, top with good-quality tonic and stir. Finish by running a lime wedge around the rim, so that citric aroma greets you as you drink, and slipping a fresh lime wedge into your perfectly made T & T (units: 1.5).

So why not sit back and savour the flavour of Tanqueray gin?

for the facts
drinkaware.co.uk

Soups

We've got a soup to suit every mood. Need cheering up? Try our comforting leek soup (page 32) or spring soup (page 35). For a fresh pick-me-up, what about the cool carrot soup (page 35) or fresh tomato broth (page 31)? And if you need to be rescued from humdrum meals, get into Indonesian soto ayam (page 27) or Japanese soba prawn tempura (page 32)

SOTO AYAM

DUCK WONTON SOUP

SOTO AYAM

This is a mad, mish-mash Indonesian soup, and you can add or subtract ingredients as you have them.

Serves 4

- 6 macadamia nuts
- 6 brazil nuts
- 3 shallots, peeled
- 2 garlic cloves, peeled
- 20g piece ginger, peeled and sliced
- 20g piece fresh turmeric, peeled and sliced, or 1 tsp ground turmeric
- 30ml peanut oil
- 20g piece fresh galangal, peeled and thinly sliced
- 2 lemongrass stalks, chopped
- 4 kaffir lime leaves, lightly crushed
- 1 litre chicken stock
- 200g rice vermicelli noodles, cooked
- 200g cooked chicken, shredded
- 4 small cooked potatoes, sliced
- 12 cherry tomatoes, halved
- 50g fresh beansprouts

To serve

- 4 hard-boiled eggs, halved
- 2 sliced fried shallots
- 4 spring onions, finely sliced

1 Put the nuts, shallots, garlic, ginger, turmeric and oil into a food processor and blend to a rough paste. Transfer to a saucepan and sauté, then add the galangal, lemongrass and lime leaves. Add the stock, bring to the boil then simmer for 15 minutes. Season with salt and black pepper. Divide the noodles, chicken, potatoes, tomatoes and beansprouts between 4 soup bowls. Pour over the broth. Top with the egg halves, shallots and spring onions.

DUCK WONTON SOUP

You could use a whole peking duck from a supermarket. If so, double the wonton ingredients and freeze any excess to use another time.

Serves 4

- ½ Chinese-style roast duck
- 8 spring onions, trimmed
- A handful of fresh coriander leaves
- 150g fresh shiitake mushrooms, caps and stems separated
- 25g piece fresh ginger, peeled
- 2 tbsp oyster sauce
- 32 wonton wrappers
- Soy sauce
- Extra chopped spring onions and coriander leaves, to serve

1 Strip the meat off the duck, discarding the skin. Put the carcass in a pot with 4 spring onions, the coriander, mushroom stems and ginger. Cover with 1.5 litres cold water. Bring to the boil, then simmer for 2 hours, skimming off any foam. Strain through a muslin-lined sieve.
2 Meanwhile, chop the remaining spring onions, the mushroom caps and the duck meat. Place in a bowl and mix with the oyster sauce.
3 Lay out 5 wonton wrappers (keep the others covered with a damp tea towel). Place 1 teaspoon of filling in each of the centres, brush the edges with water, then pinch into a purse shape. Repeat for the remaining wonton wrappers.
4 Gently heat the stock in a saucepan, season with soy and poach the wontons, in batches, for 4-5 minutes. Serve the hot broth with the wontons, chopped spring onions and coriander leaves.

ASPARAGUS SOUP & CHEESY CROUTONS

ACQUACOTTA

Recipe from Theo Randall, at the Intercontinental, London

This is a classic rustic Tuscan dish, whose name means 'cooked water'. Traditionally, farmers would put a big pot of water on the hearth in the morning. Then, as the day wore on, they would pick and add ingredients, using whatever was to hand, and the broth would be ready after work.

Serves 4

- 2 tbsp olive oil, plus extra for drizzling
- 4 celery sticks, finely chopped
- 2 small carrots, finely chopped
- 1 red onion, finely chopped
- 2 garlic cloves, 1 finely chopped, 1 halved
- 1 tsp thyme
- 200g fresh porcini or 100g dried porcini (soaked then drained), sliced
- 250g fresh plum tomatoes, skinned, deseeded and chopped
- 1 tbsp chopped parsley
- 4 slices of ciabatta
- 4 eggs

1 In a heavy-bottomed saucepan, heat the olive oil and sweat down the celery, carrot, onion, chopped garlic and thyme. Cook for 10-15 minutes, until very soft, then add the porcini and cook for another 5 minutes. Add the plum tomatoes and cook for 5 minutes more. Add 500ml water, bring up to the boil, add the parsley and season.
2 Grill the ciabatta and rub with the cut garlic halves and a drizzle of olive oil. Crack the eggs into the simmering soup and cook slowly for 2-3 minutes. Serve the soup in bowls with a slice of toasted ciabatta and an egg in each bowl.

ASPARAGUS SOUP & CHEESY CROUTONS

Serves 4-6

- 2 celery sticks, roughly chopped
- 1 onion, roughly chopped
- 1 carrot, roughly chopped
- 2 garlic cloves, roughly chopped
- Olive oil
- 400g asparagus, roughly chopped
- A big splash of white wine
- 600ml chicken or vegetable stock
- A few handfuls of spinach
- 2 tbsp double cream

Cheesy croutons
- 1 loaf of crusty bread
- Olive oil
- 3 handfuls of parmesan

1 Sauté the celery, onion, carrot and garlic in a saucepan with a good splash of olive oil and a pinch of salt. Throw in the asparagus and sweat for 10-15 minutes, until softened.
2 Meanwhile, for the croutons, preheat an oven to 180C/gas 4. Break up the crusty bread, sprinkle over some olive oil and toss with the parmesan. Pop in the oven for 5-10 minutes, until golden.
3 Add a big splash of wine to the vegetables and simmer to reduce by half. Add the stock and bring to boil. Reduce for 10 minutes. Add the spinach and cream, place in a blender and blend until smooth. Heat gently, season and serve topped with the cheesy croutons.

CLASSIC
DISH

5 MINUTE MEAL

GREEN DREAM NOODLE SOUP

Stock options

With a decent broth you can make any soup superb all year round. In spring, make a soup with onion, celery, baby leeks and veg stock; blend and stir in crème fraiche. Simmer up a summer minestrone with broad beans, courgettes and green beans. Top with pesto. Add roasted red peppers and tomatoes to hot stock, blitz, then scatter with sliced chilli and crisp bacon. In autumn, throw short pasta into chicken stock and cook till tender before adding roasted squash; blend half to thicken and top with parmesan. In the winter, combine tinned borlotti beans and tomatoes, cavolo nero, stale bread and veg stock. Drizzle with good olive oil for a Tuscan-style soup. And it's easy to cook spaghetti and frozen peas in chicken stock for noodle soup.

FRESH TOMATO BROTH

For a more substantial meal, add some cooked thin pasta or tortellini to the soup before serving, perhaps with a few baby spinach leaves.

Serves 6

- 1 x 2kg whole chicken, fat trimmed and discarded
- 4 large onions, roughly chopped
- 4 celery sticks, trimmed and roughly chopped
- 6 large garlic cloves
- 20 large mixed yellow, orange and red tomatoes (about 2.5kg in total), roughly chopped
- 1 tbsp tomato purée (optional)
- A few soft herb tips

1 Put the chicken, onions, celery, garlic and tomatoes into your largest saucepan. Add enough cold water to cover it all, pop on the lid, and bring to the boil over a high heat - about 30 minutes. Once boiling, reduce to a simmer over a medium heat with the lid askew and cook for 1 hour, or until the chicken is cooked through.
2 Carefully lift the chicken out with tongs and put aside (use the meat in the recipe for chicken with tomatoes and chorizo on page 91). Pour the soup through a fine sieve, discarding what's left behind. To further clarify it, strain through 4 layers of muslin. Have a taste to check the flavour balance and season with salt and pepper if needed.
3 Skim off the fat if serving straightaway. If you're leaving it for another time, chill, then scoop off any fat that sets on the surface. Gently reheat the soup before serving. If you think it needs a bit of a colour boost, scoop out a cup of the broth and add 1 tablespoon of tomato purée to it. Mix until well combined then return to the broth and mix again. Serve simply with a little olive oil and a few herb tips.

GREEN DREAM NOODLE SOUP

This is great with any fresh vegetables you have - just cook them till tender.

Serves 1

- 1 sachet of miso paste
- A small handful of broccoli
- A small handful of sugar-snap peas, halved
- A handful of button mushrooms, halved
- A large handful of spinach
- 1 garlic clove, sliced
- 2cm piece of ginger, grated
- 100g rice noodles, cooked
- Coriander leaves, to serve

1 Dilute the miso in a pan as per packet instructions. Simmer and add the broccoli, peas and mushrooms. Cook until the broccoli has softened and mushrooms are tender. Add the spinach, garlic, ginger and noodles and toss to warm through. Top with coriander.

VEGETARIAN

LEEK SOUP

water. Bring to the boil for 10 minutes, then remove the kombu. Return to the boil, add the bonito flakes and remove from the heat. Strain the stock through a colander lined with muslin into a bowl.
2 To make the tempura batter, lightly whisk the egg yolk, flour and 250ml iced water, using a balloon whisk.
3 To prepare the soup, reheat the stock over a low heat. Add both the soy sauces, then the noodles.
4 Meanwhile, heat an inch of vegetable oil in a wide, deep frying pan. Dip the prawns in the batter and carefully fry in the hot oil for a few minutes. Drain on kitchen paper. Transfer the stock and noodles to the bowls, add the prawns, sprinkle with the spring onions, nori and sansho and eat immediately.

FISH SOUP
Not pictured
Serves 4-6
- 1 small fennel bulb, finely chopped
- 1 leek, finely chopped
- 3 celery sticks, finely chopped
- 4 garlic cloves, finely chopped
- 2 red chillies, finely chopped
- Extra-virgin olive oil
- A small glass of white wine
- 3-4 fresh tomatoes, chopped
- A bunch of thyme, leaves picked
- 440g white fish, cut into chunks
- 400g prawns, mussels or clams

1 Gently fry the vegetables and half the chilli in a little olive oil until soft. Add 1 litre of water and the wine. Bring to the boil, then reduce the heat and simmer until the vegetables are cooked. Add the tomatoes, thyme leaves and fish. When the fish turns opaque, add the prawns, mussels or clams and simmer for 2 minutes, until the prawns are cooked and the mussels are open. Season and serve with a drizzle of olive oil and the remaining chopped chilli.

LEEK SOUP
Serves 4-6
- 1 onion, chopped
- 2 garlic cloves, chopped
- 2 tbsp butter
- 1kg leeks, trimmed and chopped
- 80g long-grain rice
- 1 tsp dried oregano
- 1.5 litres vegetable stock
- 150ml double cream
- Mixed herbs (such as parsley, dill, mint and basil), chopped, to serve

1 Sauté the onion and garlic in the butter till soft. Add the leeks and cook, stirring, for 5 minutes. Season, then add the rice and oregano and cook, stirring, for 3 minutes. Stir in half the stock. Add the rest of the stock little by little and simmer for 20 minutes. Transfer to a blender and whizz until smooth. Return to the pan, add the cream, check the seasoning and reheat. Serve sprinkled with herbs.

SOBA PRAWN TEMPURA
The ingredients for this can be found in speciality Japanese shops or online.
Serves 2
- 150g soba noodles, boiled
- 6 large tiger prawns, shelled and cleaned, tails left intact
- Vegetable oil, for frying
- 3 spring onions, trimmed and finely chopped
- 1 tbsp toasted nori, finely chopped
- A pinch of sansho spice

Dashi stock
- 40g dried kombu
- 40g bonito flakes
- 3 tbsp dark soy sauce
- 3 tbsp light soy sauce

Tempura batter
- 1 egg yolk, beaten
- 150g plain flour

1 To make the dashi, place the kombu in a saucepan and cover with 1 litre of cold

SPRING SOUP

Serves 4-6

- A large knob of butter
- 4 shallots, sliced
- 400g baby leeks, sliced
- 2 garlic cloves, finely chopped
- ½ bunch of thyme
- 400g baby carrots, halved lengthways
- 8 chicken thighs or drumsticks, skin removed and discarded
- 2 litres chicken or vegetable stock
- 250g small soup pasta
- Juice of 1 lemon

1 Melt the butter in a large pan on a low heat and sauté the shallots, leeks and garlic with the thyme sprigs till soft but not coloured - about 15 minutes. Stir in the carrots, then the chicken. Pour in the stock and bring to the boil. Season, then simmer gently for 90 minutes.
2 Using a slotted spoon, remove the chicken from the soup and set aside. When cool enough to handle, shred the meat off the bone, then return to the pan with the pasta. Cook for a further 10 minutes, or until the pasta is tender. Add lemon juice to taste.
Tip You can use leftover poached or roast chicken instead of thighs or cooked, shredded drumsticks. Just add the chicken at the end with the pasta.

VEGAN

CHILLED CARROT SOUP

CHILLED CARROT SOUP

Serves 4-6

- 600g carrots, peeled and grated
- 3 tbsp icing sugar
- 2 tbsp extra-virgin olive oil, plus extra to serve
- 2 tbsp orange-blossom water
- 500ml fresh orange juice
- ½ tsp ground cumin

1 Whizz the carrot, icing sugar, oil and orange-blossom water in a blender until smooth. Add the orange juice and blend again briefly to combine. Transfer to a large bowl, cover with clingfilm and refrigerate for a few hours. Ladle the chilled soup into bowls and serve with a sprinkle of cumin and a good drizzle of extra-virgin olive oil.

COURGETTE SOUP

Not pictured

A fresh and easy summer soup.
Serves 4

- Olive oil
- 2 onions, chopped
- 2 garlic cloves, thinly sliced
- 8 courgettes, thinly sliced
- 1 litre chicken or vegetable stock
- A bunch of mint, leaves picked
- 200ml crème fraîche
- Juice of 1 lemon

1 Heat a splash of olive oil in a large pan and sauté the onions and garlic for 10 minutes until soft and sticky. Add the courgettes, and fry for a couple of minutes then add the stock. Bring to the boil and simmer for 10 minutes or until the courgettes are cooked.
2 Add the mint leaves, season well then blitz with a hand blender. Stir through the crème fraîche and lemon juice and serve with crusty fresh bread.

TOMATO & CHORIZO SOUP

Not pictured
Serves 6

- 2 garlic cloves, thinly sliced
- A bunch of parsley, leaves picked and chopped, stalks chopped
- 200g chorizo, chopped
- Extra-virgin olive oil
- 1kg tomatoes, chopped
- 1 litre chicken or vegetable stock
- 2 x 410g tins cannellini beans, drained
- 1 loaf stale ciabatta, crusts removed, bread torn into bite-sized chunks

1 In a large pan, sauté the garlic, parsley stalks and chorizo in a little oil for about 5 minutes. Add the tomatoes and stock. Season and bring to the boil. Add the beans and simmer for 5 minutes. Mash the beans a little, then add the bread and simmer for 5-10 minutes. Stir through the parsley leaves and serve.

Pasta & rice

Those in search of a late-night snack will love punchy puttanesca (page 43), and for a satisfying lunch, whip up tuna & bean tagliatelle (page 37) or use leftover rice in a kedgeree (page 49). If it's a crowd-pleaser you're after, try our bolognese (page 40), in fact, we've got all the classics – amatriciana (page 40), pesto (page 47) and squid ink risotto (page 50)

SPAGHETTI VONGOLE

TUNA & BEAN TAGLIATELLE

SPAGHETTI VONGOLE
Serves 4 as a starter

- 250g dried spaghetti or linguine
- 1 red chilli, deseeded, finely chopped
- 2 garlic cloves, finely chopped
- A small bunch of parsley, chopped
- 250g fresh clams, washed
- 150ml white wine
- Olive oil
- 2 large plum tomatoes, diced
- Juice of 1 lemon

1 Cook your pasta in a pan of boiling salted water until al dente, then drain.
2 Meanwhile, place a large pan on a medium heat. In a bowl, mix the chilli, garlic and most of the parsley. When the pasta has 4 minutes to go, throw in the clams and half the chilli mix. Add the wine and drizzle with oil. Put the lid on and shake the pan as the clams cook. After a couple of minutes, remove the lid to check they've opened (discard any that haven't), add your pasta, tomatoes and remaining chilli mix. Add the lemon juice and cook for another minute, stirring. Serve scattered with reserved parsley.

TUNA & BEAN TAGLIATELLE
Serves 4-6

- 500g dried tagliatelle
- 400g mixed green and yellow beans

- A handful of breadcrumbs
- A small handful of grated parmesan
- Extra-virgin olive oil
- 2 garlic cloves, finely sliced
- 2 x 400g tins of chopped tomatoes
- A handful of black olives, stoned
- 1 x 500g jar or tin of tuna in oil
- A large bunch of parsley, chopped

1 Preheat the oven to 200C/gas 6. In a large pan, cook the pasta in plenty of boiling salted water, adding the beans for the final 5 minutes of cooking.
2 Meanwhile, mix the breadcrumbs and parmesan and spread it on a baking tray. Bake for 5 minutes, till golden brown.
3 In a pan, fry the garlic in a splash of oil till it takes a little colour, then add the tomatoes and cook for a few minutes. Add the olives, tuna and parsley. Season.
4 Once the pasta and beans are cooked, drain, reserving a cup of the water. Toss the pasta in the sauce, adding a little cooking liquid if needed. Serve sprinkled with breadcrumbs and drizzle with oil.

EASY MEATBALL FUSILLI
Pictured on the cover
Serves 4-6

- 400g Italian-style sausages
- Extra-virgin olive oil
- 3 garlic cloves, finely chopped

- 1-2 fresh red chillies, finely chopped
- A small bunch of flat-leaf parsley, leaves picked, stalks finely chopped
- A small bunch of fresh basil, leaves picked, stalks finely chopped
- 2 x 400g tins chopped tomatoes
- 500g giant fusilli or other twisty pasta
- Parmesan, to serve

1 Cut the skins of the sausages and remove the meat, or simply squeeze the meat out of each sausage. Shape each sausage into 3-4 meatballs. Put a wide pan on a medium heat and add a drizzle of oil. Add the garlic, chilli and herb stalks. Gently fry till the garlic and chilli soften, then add the meatballs and continue to fry, rolling the meatballs around the pan until evenly browned. After about 5-7 minutes, add the tomatoes and pinches of salt and pepper. Bring to the boil, then reduce to a simmer. Finely chop the parsley leaves and tear up some basil leaves. Once the sauce has been simmering for 10 minutes, add the chopped and torn herbs and continue to simmer for 15-20 minutes, till thickened and delicious. Taste for seasoning.
2 Meanwhile, cook your pasta according to packet instructions, reserving a mug of the cooking liquid. Stir the pasta into the sauce, adding cooking water if the sauce is too thick. Serve with grated parmesan and remaining basil leaves.

ASPARAGUS &
CRAB LINGUINE

ASPARAGUS & CRAB LINGUINE
Serves 4–6
- 500g linguine
- A large knob of butter
- Extra-virgin olive oil
- ½ tsp fennel seeds
- 1 red chilli, finely chopped
- 300g crabmeat
- 2 bunches of asparagus
- Zest and juice of 1 lemon
- Pea shoots or rocket, to serve

1 Cook the pasta according to the packet instructions. Meanwhile, melt the butter with a little oil in a frying pan. Bash the fennel seeds using a pestle and mortar till ground, then add to the pan with the chilli. Fry for a minute, then add the crab to heat through. Remove from the heat.
2 Using a peeler, shred your asparagus into long, thin strips and leave to one side. When the pasta is done, drain, reserving a cup of pasta water and add the pasta to the frying pan with the crab. Place back on a medium heat, add the asparagus and the lemon zest and juice, and toss well. Add a little pasta water to loosen if needed and season to taste. Serve with a drizzle of olive oil, topped with pea shoots or rocket.

Pasta pronto!

What could be better than pasta when you're hungry and in a hurry? Carbonara is one of the quickest. Whisk eggs, grated parmesan and black pepper in a bowl, fry bacon (or sausage meat), and tip into the eggs before pouring over hot pasta and tossing to combine. Vegetarians can use fried mushrooms. Or, gently fry sliced garlic and fresh or dried chilli in oil, then stir in parsley and a squeeze of lemon before tossing through pasta. (For a salty kick, melt anchovies in with the garlic.) To get a serve of veg, add broccoli or peas to your pasta at the end of cooking. And if you have no parmesan, fried breadcrumbs make a cheap and crunchy topping.

PAPPARDELLE WITH PEAS, BROAD BEANS & PECORINO
Serves 4–6
- 500g pappardelle
- 2 big handfuls each of broad beans (outer skins removed) and peas
- Extra-virgin olive oil
- Zest and juice of 1 lemon
- A small bunch of mint, finely chopped
- A good handful of grated pecorino, plus extra to serve

1 Cook the pasta according to the packet instructions, reserving a little cooking water. Meanwhile, blanch the beans and peas for 2 minutes. Drain, then toss with the cooked pasta, a good drizzle of olive oil, the lemon juice and zest, half the mint, the pecorino and salt and pepper to taste . Use a little cooking water to loosen if it is too dry. Top with remaining mint, a generous drizzle of olive oil and a good grating of pecorino.

10
MINUTE
MEAL

BUCATINI ALL' AMATRICIANA

RAGU ALLA BOLOGNESE

An authentic bolognese contains very little tomato, relying on the slow cooking of vegetables, wine and meat for its rich flavour and texture.

Serves 8-10

- 2 tbsp butter
- 2 tbsp olive oil
- 120g pancetta, finely chopped
- 3 garlic cloves, peeled and finely chopped
- 2 large onions, finely chopped
- 2 carrots, finely chopped
- 2 celery sticks, finely chopped
- 2 fresh bay leaves
- 400g minced beef
- 400g minced pork
- 400g minced veal
- 100g chicken livers, chopped
- 400ml white wine
- 150g tomato purée
- ½ tsp grated nutmeg
- 400ml beef or chicken stock, heated
- 1kg tagliatelle
- Grated parmesan, to serve

1 Heat the butter and olive oil in a large saucepan over medium heat and sauté the pancetta for 5 minutes, until browned. Add the garlic, onion, carrot, celery and bay leaves and sauté for 15 minutes, until softened.
2 Add the minced beef, pork and veal and cook, stirring, for about 10 minutes until browned. Add the chicken liver and cook for a further 3 minutes. Stir in the wine and cook till it evaporates - about 10 minutes. Stir in the tomato purée and nutmeg and season well. Add the stock and bring to the boil. Cover, and simmer over low heat for 1½ hours, stirring occasionally, then remove the lid and cook uncovered for a further half hour.
3 Meanwhile, cook the tagliatelle in plenty of boiling salted water until al dente. Drain and serve with a spoonful of the sauce, some grated parmesan and a good drizze of olive oil.

BUCATINI ALL' AMATRICIANA

This tomatoey sauce with a kick, from the town of Amatrice in Italy's Lazio province, is traditionally based on guanciale - cured pig's cheek - and is always served with long, hollow pasta.

Serves 4

- 3 tbsp olive oil
- 1 large onion, finely chopped
- 150g pancetta, diced
- 2 garlic cloves, finely chopped
- 75ml white wine
- 10 fresh tomatoes, peeled, deseeded and chopped, or 1½ x 400g tins (or jars) cherry tomatoes
- ½ tsp dried chilli flakes, or 1 fresh chilli, deseeded and finely chopped
- 500g ziti or bucatini pasta
- Grated pecorino cheese, to serve

1 Heat the oil in a large saucepan over a medium heat and sauté the onion for about 3 minutes, or until it is translucent and softened. Add the pancetta and the garlic and continue to cook for a further 5 minutes. When the garlic and pancetta have taken on some colour, pour in the wine and cook for another 5 minutes, or until the wine has evaporated.
2 Add the tomatoes and chilli and season to taste with sea salt. Simmer over a low heat for about 30 minutes, or until the sauce has thickened and become richer.
3 Meanwhile, cook the pasta in boiling salted water until al dente. Drain and serve with generous spoonfuls of the sauce, grated pecorino and a good drizzle of olive oil.

CROWD
PLEASER

CLASSIC DISH

SPAGHETTI PUTTANESCA

Second life

There are plenty of uses for leftover pasta. Frittatas are a great way to use cooked pasta, even if it's mixed with sauce. Place it in a pan and cover with seasoned, beaten eggs and some grated cheese. Put in a hot oven and cook till the eggs are set. Fritters are also good. Put cooked pasta in a bowl and add chopped anchovies, parsley and lemon zest, parmesan, chilli flakes and a beaten egg to bind. Fry in a hot pan till golden and crunchy. Or you can fry cold spaghetti in a little olive oil till crisp in parts, then sprinkle over salt, pepper, grated nutmeg and parmesan. For picnics, combine cooked pasta with chopped spring onion, shredded cooked chicken, peas, a squeeze of lemon and crème fraîche. Or, mix cooked pasta with tomato, olives and tinned tuna, then bake at 180C/gas 4 till hot and crisp on top.

SPAGHETTI BAKED IN PAPER

SPAGHETTI PUTTANESCA

This robust sauce is a good use of store-cupboard staples and has its origins from around Naples.

Serves 4

- 3 tbsp olive oil
- 4 garlic cloves, thinly sliced
- 750g plum tomatoes, peeled, deseeded and chopped
- 1 tsp dried oregano
- 70g drained capers, rinsed
- 80g black olives
- 1 small fresh red chilli, deseeded and chopped, or ½ tsp dried chilli flakes
- 500g spaghetti, to serve

1 Heat the olive oil in a large saucepan over a low heat and sauté the garlic until softened and turning golden. Transfer to a small bowl. Put the tomatoes and oregano in a pan and cook over a low heat for about 30 minutes, or until thickened. Season generously.
2 Add the garlic to the sauce along with capers, olives and chilli. Cook for a further 10 minutes over low heat.
3 Meanwhile, cook the pasta in plenty of boiling salted water. Drain and serve immediately with the sauce.

SPAGHETTI BAKED IN PAPER

Serves 4

- 80ml extra-virgin olive oil
- 400g prawns, peeled, veins removed, tails intact
- 300g small squid, cleaned, cut into rings with the tentacles whole
- 2 garlic cloves, chopped
- 1 birds-eye red chilli, deseeded, sliced
- 200g cherry tomatoes
- 4 tbsp salted capers, rinsed
- 180ml dry white wine
- 400g spaghetti
- Chopped parsley, to serve

1 Heat half the oil in a frying pan and sear the prawns and squid in batches for 2-3 minutes. Transfer to a bowl. Add the rest of the oil to the pan and sauté the garlic and chilli for 2 minutes. Add the cherry tomatoes and sauté for 2-3 minutes more, stirring. Add the capers and wine, season with sea salt and black pepper, and bring to the boil. Turn the heat down to a simmer.
2 Meanwhile, cook the pasta in plenty of boiling salted water for 6 minutes. Drain and add to the sauce, along with the prawns and squid.
3 Preheat the oven to 180C/gas 4. Place 2 large squares of parchment each in the centre of 4 bowls. Divide the mixture between them. Gather the paper around each pile of pasta mixture, tying the tops with kitchen twine, then transfer to a roasting tin. Bake for 15 minutes.
4 Remove and transfer each bag to a bowl. Open the bags, sprinkle over the parsley between them, and serve.

PICNIC PASTA SALAD

PASTA CON LE SARDE

With its distinctive fragrance and sweet and sour flavours, this is a Sicilian classic. Locals make it using the intensely flavoured fennel that grows wild all around the island.

Serves 4-6

- 6 baby fennel bulbs, including green tops
- 6 tbsp olive oil
- 1 onion, peeled and thinly sliced
- 1 tsp saffron threads
- 40g sultanas , raisins or currants, soaked in warm water
- 200g pine nuts, toasted
- 4 anchovy fillets
- 12 fresh sardines, cleaned and boned, heads removed, to produce butterfly fillets
- 2 tbsp toasted breadcrumbs
- 500g bucatini, to serve

1 Cook the fennel in plenty of boiling salted water for 8-10 minutes, or until it is tender. Transfer with a slotted spoon to kitchen paper to dry, then roughly chop and place in a bowl, reserving the cooking water.
2 Heat half the olive oil in a saucepan over a medium heat and sauté the onion for about 5 minutes, until softened. Add 500ml of the fennel water, as well as the saffron, sultanas and pine nuts and simmer over a low heat for 5 minutes.
3 Meanwhile, sauté the anchovies in the remaining oil in a small saucepan on a low heat for few minutes until they disintegrate, then add them to sauce.
4 Add the sardines to the saucepan and cook for 3-4 minutes, then add the fennel. Season generously with sea salt and freshly ground black pepper and cook for a further 3-4 minutes.
5 Cook the pasta in boiling fennel water until al dente. Drain and serve with the sauce, sprinkling breadcrumbs on top.

PICNIC PASTA SALAD

Serves 4-6

- 500g fusilli
- Extra-virgin olive oil
- 150g pumpkin seeds
- 1 x 190g jar red pesto
- 3 tbsp crème fraîche
- 1 x 450g jar of roasted mixed peppers
- 150g salad leaves

1 Boil a large pan of salted water and cook the pasta until al dente. Drain, rinse in cold water, and tip into a large bowl. Generously drizzle with olive oil.
2 Meanwhile, toast the seeds and add to the pasta, along with the pesto, crème fraîche and a good pinch of sea salt and black pepper. Combine well, making sure every piece of pasta is coated. Chop the peppers and stir through the pasta. If you're taking it on a picnic, transfer to a container now. Just before serving, stir through a little more extra-virgin olive oil, if needed.

PASTA CON LE SARDE

TRENETTE WITH PESTO, POTATOES & GREEN BEANS

SPAGHETTI WITH PINE NUTS, CAPERS & SULTANAS

TRENETTE WITH PESTO, POTATOES & GREEN BEANS

In Liguria, this classic recipe uses flat pasta like trenette or linguine. Traditionally, pasta, beans and potatoes were all cooked in one pot.

Serves 4-6

- 200g kipfler (or salad) potatoes, peeled and roughly chopped
- 200g green beans, topped and tailed
- 500g trenette or linguine
- Grated, parmesan, to serve

Pesto

- 2 garlic cloves, peeled
- 125g fresh basil leaves
- 4 tbsp grated pecorino or parmesan
- 2 tbsp toasted pine nuts
- 280ml extra-virgin olive oil

1 Cook the potatoes in a large pan of boiling salted water for 10 minutes or until tender, adding the beans for the final 5 minutes of cooking time.
2 For the pesto, put the garlic and 1 teaspoon of sea salt in a mortar and pound with pestle till crushed. Add the basil leaves, a few at a time, pounding to form a paste. Add the cheese and pine nuts and pound again, then slowly pour in the oil and combine well.
3 Meanwhile, cook the pasta in boiling salted water until al dente, then drain, reserving some of the cooking water.
4 Add the potatoes and beans to the pasta pan and pour in the pesto. Mix gently, adding a little pasta water to loosen if needed. Serve with parmesan.

SPAGHETTI WITH PINE NUTS, CAPERS & SULTANAS

Recipe from Jules Hunt, Jamie's Italian
Serves 4

- 400g spaghetti
- 2 tbsp olive oil, plus extra to serve
- 2 small onions, finely chopped
- 4 garlic cloves, finely sliced
- 3 fresh red chillies, finely chopped
- 16 anchovy fillets
- 2 fennel bulbs, finely chopped, tops reserved
- 1 dried chilli, crumbled
- 80g raisins
- 65g capers
- 100g pine nuts, toasted
- A small bunch of parsley, stalks and leaves chopped separately
- Zest and juice of 2 lemons

Herby breadcrumbs

- 1½ tbsp each of finely chopped thyme and rosemary
- 2 garlic cloves, finely chopped
- 4 tbsp olive oil
- 160g stale ciabatta bread, grated

1 Prepare the breadcrumbs first. In a heavy-bottomed pan, fry the herbs and garlic in the olive oil. Add the bread, season, and cook until golden. Set aside.
2 Cook the spaghetti according to packet instructions, until al dente. Drain, reserving a cup of the water. In a heavy-bottomed frying pan, heat the oil and sauté the onion and garlic until soft. Add the fresh chilli, then stir in the anchovies and cook for 1-2 minutes, until they melt. Add the fennel and dried chilli and cook for 3 minutes - don't let the mixture colour. Add the raisins, capers, pine nuts and chopped parsley stalks. Season.
3 Toss the pasta with a little reserved cooking water. Add the fennel tops, parsley leaves and lemon juice and zest. Serve topped with the herby breadcrumbs and a drizzle of olive oil.

RESCUE ME KEDGEREE

RESCUE ME KEDGEREE

This Anglo-Indian dish is perfect for breakfast, lunch or dinner – and Jamie reckons it's the best hangover cure.

Serves 4-6

- 250g basmati rice
- 4 eggs
- 2 fresh bay leaves
- 500g undyed smoked haddock fillets, skin off, bones removed
- 2 lemons
- Olive oil
- A knob of butter
- 1 onion, finely chopped
- A small bunch of fresh coriander, leaves picked, stalks finely chopped
- 1 red chilli, deseeded and finely sliced
- 1 heaped tbsp madras curry paste
- Lemon wedges, yoghurt and sliced chilli (optional), to serve

1 Bring 2 large pans of salted water to the boil. Wash the rice till the water runs clear. Add the rice to one pan and cook for 2 minutes less than directed by the cooking instructions. Add the eggs and bay to the other pan and squeeze in the juice of half a lemon. Add the squeezed lemon half to the pan, too, and leave to simmer for 7-8 minutes, adding the haddock halfway through.
2 Meanwhile, get a large frying pan on a medium heat and add a good drizzle of oil and a knob of butter. Once hot, add the onions to fry for a few minutes, then add the coriander stalks and chilli and leave them to sweat till they caramelise.
3 When the rice is cooked, drain it, and put aside. After 3-4 minutes your haddock should be flaking apart; carefully pour most of the water away. Transfer the eggs to a colander and rinse under the cold tap until they're cool. Discard the bay leaves and lemon half.
4 Add the curry paste to the onion pan, stir it through, fry for 5 more minutes, then take the pan off the heat. Tip in your rice and stir it through – don't totally mix it all together, it's nice to have a marbled effect. Roughly chop the peeled eggs and add to the pan, then flake over the haddock. Roughly chop most of the coriander leaves and add to the pan along with the juice from the remaining lemon. Gently fold everything together.
5 Put the pan on a low heat for 5 minutes

CHICKEN, LEMON & CINNAMON PILAF

until it is warm, then taste and adjust the seasoning. You shouldn't need too much as the smoked fish gives it lots of flavour. Get a fork and fold it over a few times to keep it nice and light. When you hear sizzling, take it off the heat, and scatter over the reserved coriander. Serve with some lemon wedges, yoghurt and sliced chilli, if desired.

CHICKEN, LEMON & CINNAMON PILAF

Serves 6

- 6 tbsp plain yoghurt
- Juice of ½ lemon
- 6-8 chicken breasts, cut into chunks
- About 3 tbsp groundnut oil
- A small knob of butter
- 500g basmati rice
- 2 cinnamon sticks
- 4 cardamom pods, cracked
- 1 litre hot chicken stock
- Juice and zest of 1 lemon
- A handful of pine nuts, flaked almonds, cashews or pistachios (or a mixture)
- A small bunch of fresh parsley, leaves picked and chopped

1 Mix the yoghurt and lemon juice, season, then stir in the chicken. Marinate for 20-30 minutes. Shake off the excess yoghurt, then fry the chicken in batches in a little groundnut oil over a medium heat until golden and cooked through.
2 Meanwhile, in another pan, melt the butter with 1 tablespoon of oil. Add the rice and stir until coated. Cook over a medium heat for 1-2 minutes before adding the spices, the stock, and the lemon juice and zest and season.
3 Bring to the boil, turn the heat down to low, cover, and cook for about 15 minutes, before removing the spices. Toast the nuts in a dry pan. Combine the chicken, rice, and nuts and sprinkle with the parsley. Serve with a wedge of lemon and a cold glass of white wine.

SQUID INK RISOTTO

SQUID INK RISOTTO

You can buy squid ink at good delicatessans and fishmongers.

Serves 4-6

- 750ml fish stock
- 50ml olive oil
- 1 onion, chopped
- 2 garlic cloves, chopped
- 300g squid, sliced
- 350g risotto rice
- 2 tsp squid ink
- 250ml dry white wine

1 Bring the stock to the boil, then keep hot. Meanwhile, heat the olive oil in a large saucepan and sauté the onion and garlic until softened. Add the squid, season generously with salt and pepper, and cook for 5 minutes.
2 Add the rice, squid ink and wine and cook over a medium heat until the wine reduces. Add the stock a cup at a time, stirring until each addition is absorbed. Continue in this way for 20 minutes, or till rice is al dente. Serve immediately.

With the grain

Once you've mastered a basic risotto method - as in our pea & mint risotto (right) - you can throw in whatever other ingredients you fancy. For a springtime risotto, add chopped asparagus stalks with 10 minutes' cooking left and their tips 5 minutes later. In summer, stir through thinly sliced courgette and lots of basil at the end; or 3 minutes before the end, throw in some cooked clams, a big splash of their cooking liquid, chopped parsley, and a squeeze of lemon. For a flavour of autumn, stir through roast squash, chopped sage and toasted hazelnuts. Or add some chopped wild and chestnut mushrooms at the beginning of cooking with a little chopped pancetta.

PEA & MINT RISOTTO

Serves 4-6

- A knob of butter
- 2 tbsp olive oil
- 1 large onion, finely chopped
- 2 garlic cloves, finely chopped
- 2 celery sticks, finely diced
- 400g risotto rice
- 250ml dry white wine
- 1.1 litres hot chicken or vegetable stock
- 100g peas, fresh or frozen
- A handful of mint, leaves chopped
- 100g grated parmesan

1 In a large frying pan over a low heat, melt the butter and olive oil and sauté the onion, garlic and celery for about 15 minutes, until veg are soft but not coloured. Stir through the rice and cook for 2 minutes till the grains are slightly translucent. Add the wine and stir till it has all been absorbed. Season and add a ladleful of stock at a time, stirring, then adding more when the last ladleful has been absorbed. Throw in the peas and cook until done, about 5 minutes, adding a splash of water if it gets too sticky. Take off the heat, stir though the mint and parmesan, season and serve.

PEA & MINT RISOTTO

The Single Malt Whisky Flavour Map

SMOKY

Ardbeg 10   Laphroaig 10   Lagavulin 16

          Caol Ila 12
          Talisker 10
               Bowmore 12   Talisker 18
               Highland Park 12

    Springbank 10

LIGHT   RICH

                              Cragganmore 12
          Oban 14   Bruichladdich 15
                                        Mortlach 16
  Dalwhinnie 15
    Cardhu 12   Clynelish 14   Singleton of
    Royal Lochnagar 12 Glen Elgin 12 Dufftown 12   Macallan 10

  Glenkinchie 12
    Glenlivet 12   Glenkinchie Distiller's Edition
                Glenmorangie 12
    Jura 10   Aberlour 10
          Glenfiddich 12
    Knockando 12   Bunnahabhain 12
                Scapa 14

  Glen Spey 12

DELICATE

flavour map

"Whisky isn't complicated, it's just never been explained properly," says drinks writer Dave Broom. To resolve this problem, Broom and the experts at Diageo worked together to develop the Single Malt Flavour Map. The map (above) plots the flavour of 32 whiskies, including THE SINGLETON® of Dufftown, on two intersecting axes — one a scale from light to rich, the other from delicate to smoky. "I believe the Flavour Map is a major step forward in helping people understand this magnificent spirit," says Broom. We'll drink to that!

The best possible taste

The world of whisky can be an intimidating place. With so many different whiskies to choose from, where do you begin? **THE SINGLETON® of Dufftown** has been specially created to be the single best-tasting malt whisky. A beautifully balanced, well-rounded single malt, **THE SINGLETON® of Dufftown** is both warm and approachable – making it the perfect starting point for a lifetime's exploration into the world of whisky.

Distilled in the heart of the Speyside region, **THE SINGLETON® of Dufftown** combines the pure spring waters of Highlandman John's Well with malted barley in a traditional process, which uses a longer fermentation and a slower distillation regime to produce a high-quality spirit. The single malt is then matured for 12 years in American oak bourbon barrels and European oak sherry casks for a smoother, richer flavour.

The result is a mellow single-malt whisky that will delight aficionado and newcomer alike. After all, whisky has a refined taste like olives, blue cheese or oysters – our palates are not always born liking them, we have to work at it. However, once we start to appreciate the complexity of flavours, it opens a world of satisfaction, as is the case with **THE SINGLETON® of Dufftown**.

So if you're curious to find out what all the fuss is about, let **THE SINGLETON® of Dufftown** show you just how enjoyable single-malt scotch can be.

for the facts
drinkaware.co.uk

Salad & veg

Salads are good for you, but these recipes aren't just for the health-conscious or vegetarians. Celebrate the season with an easy Roman-style spring vignole (page 56) or a delicious winter salad with ham and eggs (page 60). Thrill meat-free friends with a pretty ratatouille terrine (page 65) and jazz up Sunday roast with Jamie's veg megamix (page 69)

COURGETTE ANTIPASTO

ROAST DUCK, CHERRY & FETA SALAD

COURGETTE ANTIPASTO

This is such a simple dish to make. Serve it on a platter as a side, in sandwiches or stirred through pasta with crisp bacon.

Serves 4-6

- 750g courgettes
- ½ garlic clove
- ½ bunch of basil, leaves picked
- Extra-virgin olive oil
- Red wine vinegar

1 With a knife or a mandolin, slice the courgettes into 2-5mm-thick ribbons. Bash the garlic with a pinch of salt in a pestle and mortar. Add the basil, mash to a paste, then add a big splash of oil and a drizzle of vinegar and stir together.
2 Put a griddle pan on a high heat. When it is scorching hot, grill the courgette slices, in batches if necessary, until char marks appear across them, then remove them to a large board or plate. Toss the courgette in the basil dressing and season with salt and black pepper.

ROAST DUCK, CHERRY & FETA SALAD

Look for plum-seed oil online, or in speciality food shops. Don't worry if you can't find it, just leave it out, or add a drop of almond essence.

Serves 2 (4 as a starter)

- 2 duck legs
- 250g cherries, stoned
- 100g watercress
- 150g feta, crumbled into chunks

Vinaigrette

- 1 tbsp extra-virgin olive oil
- 1 tsp extra-virgin plum-seed oil (or an extra tsp of extra-virgin olive oil, plus 1-2 drops of almond essence)
- 1 tbsp balsamic vinegar

1 Preheat the oven to full whack. Put the duck legs on a baking tray, season, then put them in the oven to roast. Immediately turn the heat down to 180C/gas 4 and cook for about 35 minutes, until the skin is crisp and the meat is tender. Rest for 5 minutes.
2 Meanwhile, place the cherries in a salad bowl with the watercress and feta. Make the vinaigrette by mixing together the ingredients in a jar or glass. Then shred the duck meat and skin, add it to the bowl, pour over the vinaigrette, toss and serve.

CELERIAC BOULANGERE

Not pictured

Serves 6-8

- 2 onions, sliced
- 3 tbsp olive oil
- A small handful each of rosemary, thyme and sage, leaves chopped
- 1 garlic clove, halved
- 500g floury potatoes, peeled and thinly sliced
- 750g celeriac, peeled and thinly sliced
- 400ml vegetable stock
- 50g butter
- 4 handfuls of stale breadcrumbs

1 Preheat the oven to 200C/gas 6. Sauté the onions in a frying pan with a little oil and most of the herbs till soft. Rub the garlic over a baking dish. Layer the potatoes and celeriac in the dish with the cooked onions. Season, pour over the stock and top with knobs of butter. Cover with foil and bake for 45 minutes.
2 Mix the breadcrumbs with rest of the herbs and a drizzle of olive oil. After 45 minutes, remove the foil, sprinkle over the breadcrumbs and bake for a further 15-20 minutes, until golden.

POTATO, CAPERS & ROCKET SALAD

Add the stock and the frozen peas and broad beans. Stir in the drained artichokes, then a few sprigs of mint. Season with salt and pepper. Lay the slices of prosciutto over the top to form a lid, bring to a simmer and allow to bubble away gently for 10 minutes. **2** Pick the rest of the mint leaves from the stalks. Remove the prosciutto from the top, tear it up and stir it through the stew. Taste and adjust seasoning as necessary, then add a good splash of olive oil and serve with the mint leaves scattered on top.

WATERMELON & FETA SALAD

Not pictured
Serves 4-6

- 180g feta, crumbled into chunks
- 500g watermelon flesh, pips removed and cut into chunks
- 1 small red onion, finely sliced
- A bunch of mint, leaves picked
- Extra-virgin olive oil

1 Place the feta, watermelon and onion in a large bowl. Rip in the mint, leaving the smaller leaves whole. Season with freshly ground black pepper and drizzle over a little olive oil. Toss gently to combine and serve immediately.

ROAST VEGETABLE SALAD

Not pictured
Serves 2

- 3 tsp olive oil
- 1 tsp balsamic vinegar
- A small handful each of basil and mint, chopped
- 3 roasted beetroots, cut into chunks
- 1 roasted sweet potato, cut into wedges
- 2 handfuls of watercress
- 1 tsp each of pumpkin and sunflower seeds

1 Make a dressing by combining the oil, balsamic vinegar, basil and mint.
2 In a bowl, combine the beetroot and sweet potato wedges with watercress. Season and toss, then sprinkle with the pumpkin and sunflower seeds. Add goat's cheese to serve, if you like.

POTATO, CAPERS & ROCKET SALAD

This goes well with any cooked meat, but it's best with grilled sardines.
Serves 4-6

- 1.5kg mixed potatoes, such as jersey royal, charlotte or kipfler, some left whole and scrubbed, some peeled and cut into roughly equal sizes
- A small bunch of rocket
- 8 tbsp extra-virgin olive oil
- 4 tbsp red wine vinegar
- 2 tbsp capers, drained

1 Place the potatoes in a saucepan of salted water. Bring to the boil, then simmer for 20 minutes or until tender. Drain in a colander, allow to steam dry and transfer to a large serving bowl.
2 While the potatoes are still warm, add the remaining ingredients and season generously with sea salt and freshly ground black pepper. Toss to combine all the flavours and serve immediately.

EASY SPRING VIGNOLE

This is an easy take on a classic Roman seasonal stew. If you haven't got the patience to prepare artichokes, this version is for you. The prosciutto acts as a kind of lid on top of the vegetables to keep in the flavour. As the weather gets warmer, you can use fresh peas and broad beans (cook for another 10 minutes), but frozen work just as well.
Serves 8

- Olive oil
- 4 spring onions, finely chopped
- 400ml chicken or vegetable stock
- 500g frozen peas
- 500g frozen broad beans
- 1 x 290g jar artichokes, drained and halved
- A small bunch of mint
- 6 slices prosciutto

1 Heat a large nonstick pan on a medium heat, add a splash of olive oil and fry the spring onions for a couple of minutes.

EASY SPRING VIGNOLE

MOZZARELLA WITH WINTER FRUIT SALAD

BEETROOT & ALMOND SALAD

SALMON NICOISE

MOZZARELLA WITH WINTER FRUIT SALAD

Serves 4 as a starter

- 2 blood oranges
- 1 pomegranate, cut in half horizontally
- Juice of ½ lemon
- 3–4 tbsp extra-virgin olive oil
- 100g rocket
- A few sprigs of mint, leaves picked
- 4 x 120g balls of mozzarella
- 30g pecorino

1 Slice the pith and peel from the oranges, cut them in half horizontally and break into chunks. Over a bowl, bang the skin side of the pomegranate halves with a spoon until all the seeds have dropped out. Remove any bits of white membrane and put to one side.
2 Make a dressing, to taste, with the lemon, olive oil and a pinch of salt. Toss the rocket and mint in the dressing with the orange and place a little on each plate. Tear up the mozzarella and lay on the leaves with the oranges. Sprinkle with pepper. Scatter over pomegranate seeds, drizzle with olive oil, shave pecorino over the top and serve.

BEETROOT & ALMOND SALAD

Serves 4–6 as a side

- 500g beetroots
- 200ml plain yoghurt
- Juice of 1 lemon
- 50g flaked almonds
- 50g rocket

1 Place a pan of salted water on the heat and bring to the boil. Meanwhile, scrub and clean the beetroots, trim the tops and place them in the boiling water. Cook for 20–60 minutes, depending on their size. You will know that they're done when you can easily insert a skewer into them. Remove from the water and cool under running water. Slip off the skin, cut into chunks and place in a large bowl. Stir in the yoghurt, squeeze in the lemon juice, and season with sea salt and pepper.
2 Gently toast the flaked almonds in a dry frying pan on a low heat, shaking them constantly so they don't catch and burn. They should be evenly coloured after a few minutes, but there may be a few burnt ones that need to be removed. Scatter the almonds over the beetroot, followed by the rocket, gently toss to combine and then serve.

SALMON NICOISE

Serves 2

- 1–2 salmon fillets, about 300g in total
- 3 tbsp olive oil
- 1 soft round lettuce
- 200g salad potatoes, blanched
- 100g green beans, blanched
- A handful of black olives
- 4 plum tomatoes, cut into wedges
- 6 tbsp extra-virgin olive oil
- Juice of 1 lemon
- 1 tsp dijon mustard
- 1 garlic clove, finely chopped
- 2 hard-boiled eggs, halved

1 Season the salmon on both sides. Heat a frying pan with the olive oil, and fry the fish, skin-side down, for 4 minutes. Turn over and cook for a further 2 minutes, then remove the fish from the pan and set aside to cool.
2 Put the lettuce, potatoes, beans, olives and tomatoes in a big bowl. Toss with a dressing made with the extra-virgin olive oil, lemon juice, mustard, garlic, salt and pepper. Divide the salad between 2 serving bowls, flake over the fish and top with the halved eggs.

MEXICAN CORN ON THE COB

Classy dresser

Your dressing can make or break a salad. A good measure of thumb is to make one with 1 part lemon or vinegar to 3-4 parts olive oil, salt and pepper. After that you can add whatever flavours you fancy. For a garlicky kick, rub the bowl with half a garlic clove. For the bitter leaves you find in winter, balance their flavour by using balsamic vinegar or pomegranate seeds or juice in the dressing. If you're serving green salad with steak, whisk wholegrain mustard in with the oil, and for grilled chicken, make a rich sauce by incorporating crème fraiche and grated parmesan to your dressing. Adding capers and chopped anchovies to an olive-vinegar mix gives a Mediterranean feel to tomato salads, while grated raw root veg dressed with soy sauce, lime, chopped chilli and a dash of sesame oil goes brilliantly with fish.

MEXICAN CORN ON THE COB

Serves 4 as a side

- 4 corns on the cob
- 30g butter
- 1-2 red chillies, finely chopped
- 50g pecorino or lancashire cheese, grated
- 2 limes, cut into wedges

1 Boil the corn in salted water for about 5 minutes. Drain, then grill, turning every few minutes, until cooked and charred. Rub each cob with a knob of butter, then sprinkle over some chopped chilli and cheese. Serve with salt flakes and lime wedges.

WINTER SALAD WITH HAM & EGGS

The ham needs to be quite dry to grate well, so take some from the edge of a roast or get a piece and let it dry out for a while in a low oven.

Serves 4

- 12 quail eggs
- 500ml groundnut oil, plus 6 tbsp
- 1 parsnip
- 1-2 bunches of white dandelion
- 1 head of frisée lettuce
- 1 small head of radicchio
- 2 tbsp red wine vinegar
- 1 tsp English mustard
- A small bunch of chives, chopped
- 100g roast ham (in one piece)

1 Bring a pan of water to the boil and carefully drop in the quail eggs. Simmer for 3 minutes, then remove and cool. Peel and put to one side.
2 Heat 500ml groundnut oil in a saucepan over a medium heat. Peel the parsnip, then continue to shave with the peeler, catching all the shavings in a bowl. When the oil is hot, very carefully fry the parsnip shavings in batches until golden and crisp, then drain on kitchen paper.
3 Fill a clean sink or large mixing bowl with cold water. Snip the dandelion tips and the whitest curly frisée leaves into the water and wash gently. Open up the radicchio, pull out the tenderest baby leaves and tear them into small pieces. Wash and spin dry with the other leaves.
4 Make a dressing with the vinegar, mustard, 6 tablespoons of groundnut oil, salt and pepper. Mix the dressing, pour some of it over the leaves, toss to coat, and divide the salad between plates. Cut the eggs in half and lay on top. Mix the chives into the remaining dressing, and spoon a little more over the salad. Add a few parsnip crisps. Shave over the ham with a Microplane or a very sharp cheese grater and serve.

WINTER SALAD WITH HAM & EGGS

CHEAP & EASY

MINTY PEAS & AVOCADO

MINTY PEAS & AVOCADO

Serves 4-6 as a side
- 500g peas, fresh or frozen
- 3 ripe avocados, roughly chopped
- 2 large handfuls of mint leaves, torn
- Juice of 1 lemon
- 1 tsp dijon mustard
- 5 tbsp olive oil

1 Blanch the peas and refresh in cold water. Roughly chop the avocados and mix with the peas and the mint. Mix the lemon juice, mustard, olive oil and plenty of salt and pepper, pour over the peas, and toss gently to combine.

WINE-GUMMY TOMATOES

These tomatoes go wonderfully soft, sweet and sticky, and can be used in all sorts of other dishes.

Makes about 4 medium jars
- About 3.5kg large mixed tomatoes (enough to fill 2 big roasting trays)
- 8 garlic cloves, finely sliced
- Olive oil
- A handful of soft herbs, leaves picked
- About 200ml extra-virgin olive oil

1 Preheat the oven to 100C/gas ¼. Cut the tomatoes in half and lay them cut-side up in your baking trays. Sprinkle them lightly with sea salt, fleck a couple of garlic slices onto each half and drizzle the lot with olive oil. Pop them in the oven for 4 hours, or until soft and sticky. 2 Remove your tomatoes from the oven and leave to cool. Scatter with a few herbs – chives, mint, basil and fennel tops all work well – then layer them up in sterilised jars. Top up with olive oil to cover, replace the lids and keep them in the fridge where they'll sit for up to 2 weeks. These tomatoes are delicious on their own, spread over bread as a snack, or with a full English breakfast, but they're also great to to perk up a whole range of dishes (see above).

VERSATILE

WINE-GUMMY TOMATOES

RATATOUILLE TERRINE

RATATOUILLE TERRINE

Serves 6-8 as an entrée

- 3 yellow peppers
- 2 aubergines, thinly sliced
- 130ml olive oil
- 1½ tbsp fresh thyme leaves
- 6 medium courgettes, thinly sliced using a mandolin
- 800ml tomato juice
- 4 tbsp agar agar flakes (see note)
- 1 tbsp paprika
- 1 x 200g jar piquillo peppers, drained

Za'atar dressing

- 6 tbsp extra-virgin olive oil
- Juice of 1 lemon
- 2 tbsp za'atar (see note)
- 3 tbsp Greek-style yoghurt

1 On a hot grill, cook the peppers, until black and blistered. Seal in a plastic bag to cool, then remove the skin and seeds.
2 Preheat the oven to 200C/gas 6. Oil 2-4 roasting trays. Put the aubergine slices on the trays, brush with oil, sprinkle with thyme and sea salt and cook for 10 minutes until soft. Repeat for the courgettes.
3 Pour the tomato juice into a saucepan on a very low heat. Sprinkle over the agar agar (don't stir) and heat without boiling. After 5 minutes, stir, then simmer for 3 minutes to dissolve the flakes. Season well. Cool for 5 minutes.
4 Line a 26cm x 10cm x 7cm mould with clingfilm. Dip each aubergine slice in the tomato mixture, then overlap slightly to line mould bottom and sides – leave an overhang for the top. Fill gaps with a little tomato mixture. One by one, dip half the courgettes in the tomato and lay over the aubergines. Fill gaps with tomato mix and sprinkle over a little paprika. Repeat for half the yellow peppers, then piquillo peppers, then the rest of the courgettes and peppers. Fold in aubergine edges, brush with tomato mixture, cover with clingfilm, weigh down and chill overnight.
5 When set, turn out the terrine. Slice it with a very sharp knife. Whisk the dressing ingredients together, then drizzle over the slices of terrine.
Note Agar agar is a setting agent, available from Asian food shops and some supermarkets. Za'atar is a Middle Eastern thyme-based herb blend.

STUFFED CABBAGE

STUFFED CABBAGE

If you can't find sorrel or chervil, just double up on the other herbs.

Serves 6 as an entrée, 4 as a main

- 1 large savoy cabbage, outer leaves removed and discarded, boiled whole for 10-15 minutes, then drained
- 1-2 litres vegetable stock

Stuffing

- 1 tbsp olive oil
- 1 small onion, finely chopped
- 1 large garlic clove, finely chopped
- 150g swiss chard stalks, chopped
- 90g long-grain rice, boiled
- 50g vac-packed chestnuts, chopped
- 50g shelled walnuts, chopped
- 100g frozen peas, defrosted
- 1½ tbsp each chervil, parsley, sorrel, mint and tarragon, all finely chopped
- 1-2 handfuls coarse breadcrumbs
- 1 egg, beaten

Tomato salsa

- 3 tbsp olive oil
- 3 garlic cloves, finely chopped
- 1 red chilli, deseeded, finely chopped
- 700g tomato passata

1 For the stuffing, heat the oil in a frying pan, add the onion and garlic and sauté for 5 minutes. Mix in a bowl with the other stuffing ingredients.
2 Pull back the cabbage leaves and carve out the heart. Finely chop it and add to the stuffing. Season well. Place the stuffing into the cabbage and fold the leaves in to cover it. Wrap the cabbage in doubled muslin and tie with string.
3 Place in a large pan, cover with stock, top up with salted water as needed, and simmer over low heat for 1½ hours.
4 Meanwhile, for the salsa, heat the oil in a pan, add the garlic and chilli, and cook for 5 minutes till softened. Add the passata and season to taste. Simmer over a low heat until thickened.
5 When the cabbage is ready, remove from the muslin. Allow to cool slightly before serving with tomato salsa.

MUSTARD MASH

MUSTARD MASH

Serves 6-8

- 800g potatoes
- 175ml milk
- 3 spring onions, chopped
- 75g butter
- 1 tbsp each of dijon and wholegrain mustard
- 2 handfuls of parsley, chopped

1 Boil the potatoes in salted water till tender. Heat the milk with the spring onions. Drain the potatoes, then mash or crush with a ricer. Strain the milk, and add to the potatoes. Stir in the butter, dijon and wholegrain mustards, and season generously. Mash until smooth, then stir in the chopped parsley.

PERFECT ROAST POTATOES

It's always nice to be able to match up the flavours of your potatoes to those of your favourite roasts. If you use the olive oil flavour you'll need to use good Italian oil; for sweeter potatoes with their own flavour on show, use butter. If you're going to indulge, go for goose fat. You get chewier, tastier edges and a really rich and full flavour

Serves 4, with lovely leftovers

- 1.5kg maris piper potatoes, peeled
- Olive oil
- Red wine vinegar

Flavour combo 1

- Olive oil
- 1 head of garlic, broken into cloves
- A bunch of rosemary, leaves picked

Flavour combo 2

- 2-3 knobs of butter, cut into cubes
- 1 head of garlic, broken into cloves
- A bunch of sage, roughly torn
- 1 clementine

Flavour combo 3

- 2 tbsp goose fat
- 1 head of garlic, broken into cloves
- A bunch of thyme, leaves picked
- 2-3 bay leaves

1 Preheat your oven to 190C/gas 5. Cut the potatoes so they're even, about 7-8cm diameter. Wash your potatoes to rinse off extra starch then tip into a pot, cover with cold water and salt well. Bring to the boil and parboil for 6-7 minutes, then drain in a colander to steam for 3 minutes. Give it a shake to rough up the potatoes to help make them really crisp.
2 Tip your potatoes into a tray in one layer, and add your fat - olive oil, butter or goose fat - then season really well. Toss your potatoes in the fat and knock them about a little bit more. (If you know you'll be cooking a big roast the next day, you can get the potatoes to this stage the day before, cover them with clingfilm and pop in the fridge till you need them.)
3 Put your potatoes in the hot oven to cook for 30 minutes, until lightly golden and three-quarters cooked.
4 At this stage, you can use a potato masher to gently press each potato to increase the surface area - the more potato that's in contact with the pan, the crisper it will be. Whichever fat you're using, now prepare the rest of the flavourings. Add a good splash of olive oil to small bowl and add the herbs, garlic, a splash of red wine vinegar, then mix it up a bit. If using butter, peel in a few strips of clementine zest - you won't eat it but it adds an interesting flavour. Add the herb mix to your potatoes, give the pan a shake, then put back in the oven for 40-45 minutes, until crispy and golden.
5 Transfer briefly to a plate lined with kitchen paper to absorb some of the excess fat and serving piping hot.

Long & lovely

You can find leeks all year around, but in winter they're in season and particularly flavoursome. They have a subtle taste, so suit buttery and creamy sauces. Baked leeks are very easy: halve leeks vertically and horizontally and fry gently with sliced garlic cloves. Once coloured, put in an ovenproof dish with a splash of stock, double cream, thyme leaves, lemon zest and breadcrumbs tossed with parmesan. Cook in a hot oven for 20 minutes. Finely sliced leeks can be fried with pancetta or bacon and served with a pork chop, or sprinkled over pastry and topped with goat's cheese to make a tart. For grilled leeks, halve, slice into decent lengths, rub with oil, season and place in a hot griddle pan. And for a deliciously simple meal, slice them finely, fry slowly in butter till soft and sticky, season, then have on toast.

TURKISH-STYLE STEWED LEEKS

ROAST VEGETABLE MEGAMIX

Serves 4
- Olive oil

Carrots
- 500g carrots, peeled
- Juice from 1 clementine, squeezed, halves reserved
- A few sprigs of rosemary, leaves picked

Fennel
- 2 bulbs of fennel, peeled, quartered
- A few sprigs of thyme, leaves picked
- ½ lemon

Parsnips
- 400g parsnips, peeled
- A splash of white wine vinegar
- 2-3 of sprigs of sage, leaves torn
- 1 tsp honey, reserved

Beetroots
- 350g beetroot
- 2 tbsp balsamic vinegar
- A few sprigs of oregano or marjoram

Turnips
- 350g baby turnips
- 2 tsbp red wine vinegar
- 5 fresh bay leaves

1 Preheat the oven to 190C/gas 5. Before you roast your vegetables, you'll need to parboil them in salted water. The beetroot takes the longest - 20-25 minutes - so get that on first. The rest only needs 10 minutes - you can cook them all in the same pan (but not the one you're using for the beetroot, or else everything will turn red). When all your vegetables are parboiled, drain and let them steam dry, then separate them as they are going to be treated differently.
2 Mix up the vegetables with their matching flavours, except the honey. Lay them out on a large tray, keeping each vegetable type together.
3 Roast for 50-60 minutes, till they are caramelised and crunchy. Five minutes before the vegetables are ready, drizzle the honey over the parsnips. Take them out the oven, give the tray a shake, then pile the vegetables on a platter to serve.

TURKISH-STYLE STEWED LEEKS

Serves 4
- 3 tbsp olive oil
- 2 onions, thinly sliced
- ½ tbsp dried oregano
- 1 tsp ground cumin
- 12 leeks, trimmed, halved widthways
- 300g tomato passata
- 400ml chicken stock

1 Heat the olive oil in a large saucepan over a medium heat. Sauté the onions, oregano and cumin until soft. Add the leeks and cook for 5 minutes. Add the tomato passata and chicken stock, cover with greaseproof paper and simmer for 40 minutes, until the sauce thickens and the leeks are tender.

Fish & seafood

Push the boat out and take these wonderful ways of enjoying fish on board. Mackerel is great stuffed and grilled (page 71) or baked in a pie (page 75). Speaking of grills, seafood is beautiful on a barbie (page 72). Roasted monkfish (page 76) is an impressive dinner party dish, and small fry love fish fingers (page 86)

SALMON WITH YOUNG GARLIC & TOMATOES

STUFFED BBQ MACKEREL

SALMON WITH YOUNG GARLIC & TOMATOES

Serves 4

- Olive oil
- 1 head of fresh young garlic, sliced in thin wedges (if you can't find young garlic, substitute with 2 chopped garlic cloves and 1 sliced fennel bulb)
- 1 punnet cherry tomatoes, squashed
- 4 salmon fillets
- ½ lemon, cut into thin slices
- A handful each of chopped mint and dill

1 Place a frying pan on a medium-hot hob and add a good drizzle of oil. Throw in the garlic and fry until it softens and caramelises. Add the tomatoes and cook until they soften.
2 In another pan, heat a little olive oil on a medium heat. Season the salmon and cook, skin-side down, for 3 minutes. Turn over the fillets, add the lemon slices to the pan, and cook for another 2 minutes, or until the salmon is done to your liking. Transfer the salmon to plates, stir the mint and dill through the sauce in the pan, then tip the sauce over the salmon and serve.

STUFFED BBQ MACKEREL

Serves 4

- A handful of pine nuts, toasted
- A knob of butter
- Olive oil
- 2 red onions, finely sliced
- 2 celery sticks, finely sliced
- A few sprigs of rosemary, leaves picked and chopped
- 5 tbsp red wine vinegar
- A handful of sultanas
- A splash of red wine
- 2 ripe tomatoes
- 4 whole mackerel, gutted

1 In a large frying pan, toast the pine nuts till golden, then put to one side. Melt the knob of butter with a little olive oil and sauté the onion and celery with the rosemary leaves for 10-15 minutes, or until softened and starting to caramelise. Add the vinegar and sultanas to the pan, then, after a minute, add a splash of red wine. Chop the tomato and add to the pan and season generously with salt and pepper. Reduce the heat to a low and simmer for 15 minutes until thickened. Remove from the heat, add the pine nuts and leave to cool.
2 Lay your mackerel on a tray, rub with some olive oil, then stuff the belly with the onion-and-pine nut mixture. Season the skin of the fish, then cook on a preheated barbecue or griddle pan for 8 minutes, or until it is crisp, charred and cooked through. Serve with a mixed-leaf salad and a wedge of lemon.

LOBSTER BANANA

LOBSTER BANANA

This is a great way to cook lobster, baked in the semi-moist environment of the banana leaf (or tin foil if you can't find them). To prepare the lobster, dispatch it, then cut lengthways down the back of its tail. Remove the dark food sacs and you're ready to go. To feed four, get two 700–800g lobsters and cook them for a little longer.

Serves 2

- 2 banana leaves (or tin foil)
- 2 x 450g lobsters, tails only, halved
- 4 spring onions, finely sliced
- 2–3 mixed fresh chillies (to taste), finely sliced
- A bunch of coriander, finely sliced
- Olive oil
- 2 limes, quartered
- 120ml coconut milk
- A few wooden cocktail sticks, soaked

1 Preheat a barbecue or griddle pan so it's really hot. Open out the banana leaves or 2 double sheets of foil, each to a size slightly smaller than a tea towel. Put 2 lobster-tail halves in the middle of each and season. Divide the spring onions, chillies and coriander between the parcels. Drizzle with olive oil, then place 3 lime quarters in each parcel and squeeze the remaining quarters over the lobster. Drizzle half the coconut milk in each, then roll and fold up securely to make a pouch, securing the ends of the parcels with the soaked cocktail sticks.
2 Put the parcels on the hot barbecue or griddle pan to cook for about 7 minutes on each side. The outside will burn and cinder, but inside it will be cooked to moist perfection. Eat straight out the banana skins with a squeeze of lime.

BARBECUED OYSTER SKEWERS

Makes 4 skewers

- 20 oysters, shucked
- Finely grated zest of 1 lemon
- A few sprigs of thyme, leaves picked, plus a small bunch tied with string
- 10 slices of pancetta or smoked streaky bacon
- Extra-virgin olive oil
- Soda bread and green salad, to serve
- A few metal skewers

1 Toss the oysters in a bowl with the lemon zest and thyme, and season with black pepper. Stretch the pancetta slices using the back of a knife, then cut in half. Use them to wrap the oysters, then thread onto the skewers.
2 Barbecue or grill the skewers – adding the thyme bundle for fragrance – for about 2 minutes on each side, brushing with a little oil. Serve with bread, salad and a good squeeze of lemon.

BARBECUED OYSTER SKEWERS

CROWD PLEASER

FISH CURRY

FISH CURRY
Serves 8

- 1 butternut squash, skin on, cut into wedges
- 2 tsp cumin seeds
- 2 dried red chillies, finely chopped
- 2 tsp brown mustard seeds
- 1 tsp fenugreek seeds
- 2 tsp ground turmeric
- 15 curry leaves
- 2 tsp ground coriander
- 2 tsp chilli powder
- Olive oil
- A large piece of ginger, finely chopped
- 4 garlic cloves, finely chopped
- 1 large onion, diced
- 2 fresh red chillies, finely chopped
- 1.5kg tomatoes, roughly chopped
- 2 x 400ml tins coconut milk
- 4 tsp tamarind paste
- 16 tiger prawns, tail on
- 800g monkfish, boned and skinned, cut into 3cm chunks
- 4 red mullet fillets, halved diagonally

Garnish
- A large bunch of coriander, chopped
- 1 fresh red chilli, finely sliced
- Fresh coconut shavings

1 Preheat the oven to 200C/gas 6. Lay the squash in a roasting tray and toss with the cumin, dried chillies, 2 tablespoons of olive oil and a little salt. Roast for 40 minutes, until tender.
2 In a little oil on a medium-high heat, fry the mustard seeds, fenugreek, turmeric, curry leaves, coriander and chilli powder for a few minutes, stirring, till fragrant. Turn the heat down slightly and add the ginger, garlic, onion and fresh chilli and fry till softened. Add the tomatoes, bring to a boil and simmer for 10 minutes. Add the coconut milk and tamarind, then simmer for 10 minutes more. You can cook the curry to this stage in advance.
3 When you're ready to eat, return the curry to the boil, adding a little water if needed. Stir in the prawns, monkfish and squash. Lay the mullet on top, cover with a lid and simmer for 10 minutes. When the fish is cooked, transfer to a serving dish, scatter with fresh coriander, sliced chilli and shaved coconut. Serve with lime wedges, crunchy pickles, sautéed green beans and rice or Indian breads.

STARGAZY PIE

STARGAZY PIE
This Cornish dish, traditionally made with pilchards, gets its name because of the way the fish's heads peep out through the pie crust and appear to be looking skyward.
Serves 4

- 500g shortcrust pastry
- 4 hard-boiled eggs, plus 1 egg
- A splash of milk
- A handful of breadcrumbs
- 2 onions, finely chopped
- A large handful of parsley leaves
- 4 mackerel, gutted and boned
- 50g butter
- 4 rashers streaky bacon, chopped
- 2 tbsp plain flour
- 150ml white wine
- 400ml fish stock

1 Preheat the oven to 180C/gas 4. Roll out the pastry to 5mm thick. Whisk the single egg with the milk and brush over the rim of your pie dish. Mix the breadcrumbs with half the onion and half the parsley. Season the fish and stuff with the breadcrumb mixture.
2 Melt the butter in a frying pan and sauté the remaining onion and bacon for about 10 minutes until golden. Stir in the flour till well combined, then gradually add the wine and bring to the boil. Add the stock and season. Return to the boil again and simmer for 5–10 minutes until slightly thickened.
3 Lay the fish in the dish with their heads on the rim so they gaze upwards. Chop your hard-boiled eggs into small chunks and add to the sauce with the remaining parsley. Spoon it over the fish and put the pastry lid in place, pressing it down between the fish heads and the rim, making a crinkled effect. Brush with the egg wash and bake for 35–40 minutes.

ROAST MONKFISH IN BACON

- 2 tsp freshly grated ginger
- ½ red chilli, chopped
- Vegetable oil

1 In a food processor, whizz together the prawns, pollack, cornflour, spring onions, coriander, grated ginger, chopped red chilli, salt and pepper. Shape the mixture into 6 cakes.
2 Heat a splash of vegetable oil in a frying pan and fry for 2-3 minutes on each side till golden. Serve with a salad.

MISO-GLAZE SALMON
Not pictured
Serves 2

- 175g white miso
- 3 tbsp sake
- 50g caster sugar
- 3 tbsp mirin
- 2 x 150g salmon fillets, skin on
- Steamed greens, to serve

1 Mix the miso, sake, sugar and mirin in a heatproof bowl and place over a pan of simmering water for 30 minutes. Allow to cool. Place the salmon in a sealable bag with the glaze; marinate for up to 24 hours. Grill for 3-4 minutes, till sticky. Serve with steamed greens.

ROAST MONKFISH IN BACON
Serves 4

- 1 monkfish tail, about 1.4kg
- 14 rashers of streaky bacon
- 4 fresh bay leaves
- 3 garlic cloves, sliced
- 1 tbsp olive oil

1 Preheat the oven to 200C/gas 6. Wrap the monkfish in the bacon, inserting bay leaves and garlic slices under the bacon. Tie with kitchen string, place on a baking tray, drizzle with oil and season with pepper and salt. Roast for 40 minutes or till the bacon turns golden and crisps up, and the fish is cooked.

MONKFISH WITH SPINACH & FETA
Serves 2

- 2 x 150g monkfish fillets
- 1 tsp cumin seeds, crushed

- 2 sprigs fresh thyme, leaves picked
- 1 x 100g bag spinach, sautéed
- 100g feta, crumbled
- 1 lemon, halved

1 Sprinkle the monkfish fillets with the cumin seeds, thyme leaves, sea salt and ground black pepper. Add a little olive oil to a hot frying pan and fry for 3-4 minutes each side, until cooked. Serve on top of the sautéed spinach, then sprinkle with the crumbled feta and a good squeeze of lemon juice.

THAI-STYLE FISHCAKES
Not pictured
Serves 2

- 8 raw prawns, peeled
- 100g pollack fillet
- 3 tbsp cornflour
- 2 spring onions, chopped
- A small bunch of coriander

POACHED SALMON
Not pictured
Serves 4-6

- A side of salmon
- A small bunch of carrots, peeled
- ½ bunch of parsley,
- 2 celery sticks
- 2 bay leaves
- 1 red onion, cut into wedges
- A small pinch of black peppercorns
- ¼ bottle white wine
- Mayonnaise, to serve

1 Place the salmon in a fish kettle with the carrots, parsley, celery, bay leaves, onion and black peppercorns. Add cold water and white wine to cover and poach, covered, for 20-30 minutes over a medium heat. Allow to cool before serving warm or cold with mayonnaise.

MONKFISH WITH SPINACH & FETA

TUNA PANZANELLA

Recipe from Andrew Parkinson, Fifteen

This summery salad is delicious with any chargrilled fish or meat.

Serves 4

- 1 garlic clove, halved
- 400g stale, dense country bread, torn into chunks
- 800g mixed tomatoes (vary the sizes and colours), roughly chopped
- 1 red onion, diced
- 30g small capers, washed
- A bunch of fresh basil, leaves picked, larger ones torn
- Extra-virgin olive oil
- Red wine vinegar
- 4 x 150–200g fillets of tuna loin
- 4 tsp pesto (optional)

1 Rub the cut garlic inside a large mixing bowl, then add the bread, onion, capers, tomatoes and basil and mix. Add a good splash of oil and vinegar and season generously. Leave the salad to soak up the flavours while you cook the fish. **2** Heat a grill or frying pan till very hot. Season and lightly oil the tuna. Cook for 3–4 minutes on each side, depending on the thickness and how you like it. Spoon a generous amount of panzanella on 4 plates, place the tuna on the salad and finish with a spoonful of pesto, if you like, along with a drizzle of olive oil.

CRAB & CORN CAKES

Serves 2

- 300g mixed brown and white crabmeat
- 2 spring onions, finely chopped
- 1 chilli, finely chopped
- 3 tbsp cornflour
- Kernels from 1 cob of sweetcorn
- Plain flour, for dusting
- 4 tbsp mayonnaise
- 2 tbsp chilli sauce

1 In a bowl, mix the crab, chilli, spring onion, cornflour, sweetcorn and season. Shape into 4 medium-sized patties and coat in a little plain flour. Pan-fry in oil for 2–3 minutes each side. Mix together the mayonnaise and chilli sauce and serve with the crab cakes and lemon wedges.

Shelling out

Our crab and corn cakes are only one of many uses for crabmeat. Make a classic linguine al granchio by stirring a mix of brown and white meat through a simple tomato sauce, sprinkling over chilli and basil, and tossing with pasta. Or add it to a basic risotto towards the end of cooking – leave out the cheese, adding lemon juice and parsley instead. Stir brown meat through a broth, flavoured with saffron and fennel and thickened with cream, to make a rich bisque. Mix white meat with olive oil and basil and use to fill an avocado half for a retro light lunch. Alternatively, fry some bashed fennel seeds and dried chilli flakes in a little oil, then stir through crabmeat till warmed, and have on toast. Plainest of all, mix white crabmeat with some mayo, and enjoy in a sandwich.

LOBSTER BURGER

JAMIE LOVES IT

Best-shellers

Sweet, meaty scallops can be found at fishmongers throughout their July till December season and can be turned to a host of delicious uses – but be careful not to overcook them. Do as the Chinese do and stir-fry with strips of fresh ginger and spring onions and oyster sauce and serve with noodles. Or pan-fry pieces of black pudding till crisp, throw in some scallops for a minute or two and serve with an apple purée. Also, the sweetness of small scallops pairs beautifully with pea purée. Skewer them with chunks of salmon and cook on a barbecue, or grill some with chorizo and tomatoes before tossing with rocket. For an old-school starter, slather them on the half-shell in a sauce of garlic, parsley, shallots, garlic, cream and cheese, top with breadcrumbs and put under a hot grill to make coquille st jacques.

LOBSTER BURGER

Although you won't find lobsters in supermarkets, you'll be able to get them from any decent fishmonger. This recipe only uses the tail meat, but feel free to use the claws, too.

Serves 4

- 2 x large lobster tails
- Olive oil
- 1 heaped tsp dijon mustard
- 4 rashers of smoked streaky bacon
- 4 burger buns
- 1 garlic clove, halved
- Ketchup, mayonnaise, lemon juice, watercress, soft lettuce leaves and finely sliced red onion, to serve

Grated tomato salsa

- 2 ripe tomatoes
- ½ fresh red chilli
- Extra-virgin olive oil
- Red wine vinegar

1 To make the salsa, put a coarse grater over a chopping board and grate your tomatoes to a slurry. You'll end up with seeds and skin on one side, slurry on the other. Discard the seeds and skin. Grate in the chilli and season. Add a big splash of oil and a swig of vinegar.
2 Cut the lobster into 2cm slices (use the rivets of the tail as guides). Leave the shell on to protect the meat as it cooks and help it keep its shape. Toss the slices in oil, salt, pepper and mustard, then barbecue or grill for 2–3 minutes on each side until cooked; peel. Barbecue or grill the bacon, turning after a couple of minutes, till crisp and golden. Toast the buns at the same time, then lay the bottom halves on a board. Rub the cut garlic over each one, drizzle with oil, and add a tiny blob of ketchup, a teaspoon of mayonnaise and a squeeze of lemon.
3 Put a nice handful of watercress and lettuce on each bun. Top with lobster, salsa and red onion, crumble over the bacon and replace the bun lid. Secure the burgers with skewers to serve.

SCALLOPS & QUAIL EGG SALAD

This is a really decadent lunch that takes moments to prepare.

Serves 4

- 6 tbsp olive oil
- 200g small scallops
- 1 tsp paprika
- Juice of 1 lemon
- 1 small red chicory, thinly sliced
- A handful of lamb's lettuce
- A handful of rocket
- 8 quail eggs, boiled and halved

1 Heat half the olive oil in a large frying pan over medium heat. Season the scallops and fry for 2 minutes, until golden on each side. Add the paprika, stir and cook for another minute more. Squeeze in the lemon juice and stir.
2 Place the lamb's lettuce and rocket in a bowl. Throw in the scallops and quail eggs, plus the frying-pan juices. Add the remaining oil, toss together and serve.

OYSTER OMELETTE

OYSTER OMELETTE

Serves 1

- 1 tbsp vegetable oil
- 4 spring onions, finely sliced
- 1 red chilli, deseeded and finely sliced
- 3 eggs, beaten and seasoned
- 6 oysters, shucked
- Fresh coriander leaves and sesame oil, to serve

1 Place a 15cm omelette pan on a medium-hot heat. Add a little oil, the spring onions and chilli and cook, stirring, till they soften slightly. Pour in the eggs, tilting the pan so they cook evenly.
2 When the omelette looks half-cooked, add the oysters, then tilt the pan to redistribute any very liquid egg, then quickly flip one side of the omelette into the centre so it's doubled over. Leave the pan briefly on the heat so the oysters warm a little and the remaining egg is cooked, then quickly slide onto a plate. Serve scattered with coriander leaves and a little drizzle of sesame oil.

MIXED POKE

MIXED POKE

This popular Hawaiian dish fuses Asian flavours, such as soy, ginger and seaweed, with raw fish.

Serves 4-6

- 250g sashimi-grade sustainable tuna, cut into 1cm pieces
- 250g sashimi-grade mackerel, sea bass or kingfish, cut in 1cm pieces
- 2 tbsp toasted nori seaweed, finely shredded or crushed
- 1 tbsp freshly grated ginger
- 1 tbsp sesame seeds, toasted
- 1½ tbsp soy sauce
- ½ tbsp extra-virgin olive oil
- Sliced fresh seaweed (optional)
- Lavosh-style crispbread, to serve

1 Mix the ingredients in a large glass or a plastic bowl, cover and marinate in the fridge for 5 minutes. Sprinkle with some sliced fresh seaweed, if you can find some. Serve with lavosh-style crispbread and eat immediately.

COD WITH GARLIC, BAY & SPINACH

Not pictured

Serves 2

- Olive oil
- 2 cod steaks, about 175g each
- 2 garlic cloves, sliced
- 2 bay leaves
- A pinch of paprika
- 1 x 100g bag spinach, steamed
- 2 lemon wedges, to serve

1 Heat a splash of olive oil in a saucepan. Season and pan-fry the cod with the garlic, bay and paprika. Serve with the steamed spinach and a wedge of lemon.

SPANISH-STYLE PRAWNS

Not pictured

Serves 2

- Olive oil
- 2 garlic cloves, finely sliced
- 1 bulb of fennel, sliced
- A few sprigs of parsley, leaves picked and roughly chopped, stalks chopped
- 750g cherry vine tomatoes, halved
- A large glass of white wine
- 10 large raw prawns, butterflied, with tails left on
- 1 lemon, halved, and some good-quality bread, to serve

1 Heat a good splash of olive oil in a saucepan and gently fry the garlic till golden. Add the fennel and parsley stalks, then reduce the heat to low and sauté for 10 minutes, until softened but not coloured. Add the cherry tomatoes and wine. Bring to the boil, then simmer for 5-10 minutes, until thickened. If it's too thick, add a splash of water. Add the prawns and cook for 4 minutes, or until they're cooked and pink. Stir through parsley leaves and season. Serve with lemon and a wedge of bread.

SEARED PRAWNS WITH SICILIAN SALSA

PRAWN & EGG CURRY

SEARED PRAWNS WITH SICILIAN SALSA

Rather than chopping and slicing the ingredients for the salsa by hand, you can make it in a food processor to save time. If you do, though, try not to blitz it to a purée – it's those chunky bits that really help give it all that great character and flavour.

Serves 4 as a starter

- 1 tsp sweet paprika
- 2 garlic cloves, chopped
- Olive oil
- 16 raw king prawns, peeled but tails intact, then butterflied
- A large knob of butter
- Juice of 1 lemon
- A handful of raisins
- A handful of pine nuts
- A bunch of fresh dill or fennel tops

Sicilian salsa

- 300g red tomatoes, deseeded and finely chopped
- 2 spring onions, finely sliced
- 1cm-piece ginger, finely grated
- 1 red chilli, deseeded and finely chopped
- A small bunch of coriander, leaves picked and roughly chopped
- Juice of 2 limes
- Red wine vinegar
- Extra-virgin olive oil

1 First make the salsa. Add the tomatoes, spring onions, ginger, chilli, coriander and lime juice to a bowl with a dash of vinegar and a couple of splashes of extra-virgin olive oil. Season well.

Give it a taste to check that the flavour balance is right and add a little bit more of anything you think it might need. **2** Mix the paprika and the garlic with a good pinch of salt and pepper and 2 tablespoons of olive oil. Throw in the prawns and mix until they're coated with all the flavours. Put a large frying pan on a high heat. Add the butter and a drizzle of olive oil. Once sizzling, add the prawns and lemon juice. Cook for 2-3 minutes, turning halfway, until they take on a good bit of colour. At this point, add the raisins and pine nuts and tear in most of the dill or fennel. Toss for a further minute or so until the prawns are cooked and are sticky. **3** Spread your salsa over a large platter, use tongs to transfer the prawns on top, then scatter over the pine nuts and raisins, then tear up the remaining dill or fennel and scatter over the top. Or you can serve the prawns straight out the pan with the salsa on the side.

PRAWN & EGG CURRY

Serves 2

- 2 onions, finely sliced
- 1-2 garlic cloves, finely sliced
- 1 tsp grated fresh ginger
- Vegetable oil
- 1 tsp ground cinnamon
- 1 tsp cumin
- 8 large raw prawns, shell on
- 200ml chicken or veg stock
- 3 eggs, hard-boiled and halved
- ½ lime
- 1 red chilli, julienned
- Boiled rice, to serve

1 Fry the onions, garlic and grated ginger in a little vegetable oil until golden. Add the cinnamon and cumin, and season. Cook for 1 minute, then add the prawns and stock. Simmer for 8 minutes, then add the hard-boiled eggs and a squeeze of lime. Top with the red chilli and serve with rice or Indian-style flatbreads.

KIDS LOVE IT

FISH FINGERS, CHIPS & TARTARE SAUCE

For small fry

Fish fingers are just one great way to get kids to like fish. Make fishcakes by mashing cooked salmon or white fish with potato, spring onion and crème fraîche, coat in breadcrumbs and fry. Add chunks of pollack to a coconutty korma – don't be afraid of kids eating spices, just cut down on the chilli – or bake white fish steaks in a cheese sauce and serve with peas. Sauté chopped onion, celery and fennel with bay leaves and oregano, add a tin of tomatoes cook for 30 minutes. Lay on some fish fillets for the last five and finish with lemon. Everyone loves fish pie – and it's a great way to use leftovers. Flake cooked fish into an ovenproof dish. You can even add prawns or mussels. Gently toss the fish in a little chopped parsley and white or tomato sauce. Top with mashed potato and bake in a medium oven till hot through.

FISH FINGERS, CHIPS & TARTARE SAUCE
Serves 4
- 2 sweet potatoes
- Olive oil
- 100g plain flour
- 2 eggs
- 1 tbsp milk
- 150g breadcrumbs
- 400g firm, white fish fillets, such as pollack, skin removed

Easy tartare sauce
- A handful each of capers and gherkins
- A small handful of parsley leaves
- 150g mayonnaise
- Grated zest and juice of 1 lemon

1 Preheat the oven to 200C/gas 6. Bring a saucepan of salted water to the boil. Scrub the sweet potatoes, slice them in half lengthways, then cut into wedges. Transfer the wedges to the boiling water and parboil for 5-8 minutes until just tender. Drain in a colander and allow to dry. Place on a baking tray, drizzle with olive oil and season, then set aside until ready to bake.
2 Spread the flour on a plate. In a bowl, beat the eggs with the milk. Mix the breadcrumbs with a pinch of salt on a plate. Slice the fish fillets into strips about 2cm thick. Dip the fish in the flour, shake off the excess, dunk in the egg mix then roll in the crumbs. Place on oiled baking trays, and bake for 25-30 minutes, until the fish is cooked through and the breadcrumbs are golden. Put the sweet potato wedges in at the same time as your fish – they should take the same amount of time.
3 For the tartare sauce, finely chop the capers, gherkins and parsley and mix with the mayonnaise in a bowl. Or you can blitz it all up in a food processor. Add the lemon zest and juice, mix well and season to taste. Serve with the fish fingers and the sweet potato wedges.

SALT & PEPPER SQUID
Serves 4-6
- 750g baby squid, tentacles left whole and body tubes cut into thick rings
- 1 tsp each of sichuan, black and white peppercorns
- 1 tsp sea salt
- 6 tbsp cornflour
- 1.5 litres vegetable oil
- 2 garlic cloves, sliced
- 1 red chilli, sliced
- 4 spring onions, sliced
- 1 lime, cut into wedges, to serve

1 Dry the squid thoroughly with kitchen paper. Crush the peppercorns and salt in a mortar. Mix with the cornflour.
2 Very carefully, heat the oil in a pan to 180C. In batches, coat the squid in the cornflour mix, shaking off excess. Gently lower the squid into the oil and deep-fry until golden and crisp. Drain on kitchen paper. Fry the garlic, chilli and onion till golden. Serve it all with lime wedges.

The gold and the white

They know a thing or two about rum in Venezuela. There, in the town of Ocumare del Tuy, near the country's Caribbean coast, they've been making Pampero since 1938. Happily for us, they've not been keeping it all for themselves.

Pampero is a harmonious blend of Venezuelan rums of different ages, matured in oak casks, and named after the thunderstorm that rolls in over the South American plains. The flagship rum in the range, Pampero Especial (far left) is the original Venezuelan añejo, or aged, rum. Golden in colour, its rich, complex flavour makes it good drunk simply on the rocks, or why not try it with Coke and lime in a Cuba Libre?

Pampero Blanco, as its name suggests, is a crystal-clear white rum. All the same, it's been aged for two years to give a more rounded flavour than you'd expect. Blanco's bright, welcoming character lends itself well to cocktails, such as the classic Caribbean Mojito (pictured). It's simple to make. In a highball glass, muddle together 2 tsp brown sugar and the juice of half a lime using the back of a wooden spoon till the sugar starts to dissolve. Add a sprig or two of mint and muddle some more, then half fill with ice, pour over a measure of Pampero Blanco and top with soda.

Whether you prefer Especial's depth and complexity or Blanco's invigorating freshness, one thing is certain. By choosing Pampero you'll be plugging into a tradition of excellence that stretches back over 70 years, and which rum lovers the world over are happily cottoning on to.

for the facts
drinkaware.co.uk

Poultry & game

Why did the chicken cross the road? It saw you coming armed with these delicious poultry and game recipes! There's irresistible crispy duck salad (page 98), Jamie's flying steak sandwich (page 97) and earthy rabbit stew (page 101), not to mention glorious coq au riesling (page 101). Who can blame it?

ONE-TRAY BAKE

CHICKEN WITH TOMATOES & CHORIZO

ONE-TRAY BAKE

This is so easy – just chuck everything in one tray, then bung it in the oven.

Serves 4-6
- 1 small ciabatta loaf
- 8 chicken thighs or drumsticks
- 2 handfuls of cherry tomatoes
- A bunch of basil, leaves picked
- 1 head of garlic, broken into cloves, unpeeled
- A handful of black olives, stoned
- Olive oil
- 1 dried red chilli
- 8 slices of pancetta, or thinly sliced smoked streaky bacon

1 Preheat the oven to 180C/gas 4. Get a deep roasting tray big enough to fit all the chicken in one layer. Rip the ciabatta into medium-sized chunks and place in the tray with the chicken, tomatoes, basil, garlic cloves and olives. Add a generous drizzle of olive oil, a pinch of salt and pepper and the chilli. Toss to mix up well, then reposition the chicken on top. Bake in the oven, turning the chicken after 30 minutes.
2 After another 30 minutes, drape the pancetta or bacon on top of the chicken and return to the oven for 15 minutes, until the chicken is cooked and falling off the bone. Serve with a green salad.

CHICKEN WITH TOMATOES & CHORIZO

If you don't want to poach a whole bird you can use any leftover chicken you might have and scale down the other ingredients accordingly.

Serves 6
- 1 yellow pepper
- 1 orange pepper
- Olive oil
- 1 onion, finely sliced
- 4 garlic cloves, finely sliced
- 1kg mixed tomatoes, roughly chopped
- 1 heaped tsp sweet paprika
- 1 red chilli, deseeded and finely sliced
- A few sprigs of oregano, leaves picked and chopped (or 1 tbsp dried oregano)
- 1 poached chicken
- 200ml chicken stock
- 2 fresh chorizo sausages (about 250g)
- 1 heaped tsp fennel seeds, crushed
- Extra-virgin olive oil
- 2 heaped tbsp crème fraîche
- 2 tbsp balsamic vinegar
- Warm flatbreads or tortillas, or jacket potatoes, to serve

1 Blacken the peppers over a gas flame or under the grill, then pop them in a bowl covered with clingfilm to steam. After 15 minutes, they should peel easily; discard the skin and the seeds.
2 Heat a little oil in a large frying pan on a medium heat. Once hot, add the onion and fry for a couple of minutes, then throw in the garlic, tomatoes, paprika, chilli and most of the oregano. Cook for about 5 minutes, or until starting to soften. Meanwhile, pull the chicken off the bones in chunky pieces. Discard the bones and skin. Add the chicken to the pan with the stock. Tear the peppers into strips and add to the pan. Stir well. Leave to bubble away for 25 minutes, or till sauce has reduced and thickened.
3 Put a second frying pan on a high heat. Remove the skins from the chorizo and break the meat into rough chunks. Add a splash of olive oil to the pan, then add the sausage meat and the fennel seeds. Stir with a wooden spoon, squashing and breaking the meat into crumbs. Cook for about 5 minutes, stirring, or until dark golden, crisp and smelling fantastic.
4 Add a good splash of olive oil and a generous pinch of salt and pepper to your chicken pan. Take the pan straight to the table, dollop over the crème fraîche, drizzle with the balsamic vinegar and scatter with the crisp chorizo and reserved oregano. Serve with warm flatbreads or tortillas, or use as a topping for jacket potatoes.

LEMONY DUCK WITH ROCKET SALAD

LEMONY DUCK WITH ROCKET SALAD

Serves 1

- 1 duck breast
- A pinch of ground allspice
- A pinch of ground white pepper
- Juice of 1 lemon
- A large handful of rocket
- ¼ white onion, finely sliced
- ¼ lemon, peeled and chopped
- Olive oil

1 Slash the skin of the duck breast 3 or 4 times with a sharp knife, then rub the allspice and white pepper into the skin. Sprinkle with sea salt and transfer to a bowl. Squeeze over the lemon juice and marinate for 30 minutes.
2 Heat a barbecue or griddle pan until hot and grill the duck, turning occasionally, for 15–20 minutes. Rest the meat for 5 minutes before slicing.
3 Toss the rocket, onion and lemon segments with oil. Season and serve.

HAINANESE CHICKEN RICE

A comforting chicken and soup, with a flavour wallop from the ginger sauce.

Serves 6

- 6 shallots, peeled
- 10 garlic cloves, peeled
- 4 lemongrass stalks, chopped
- 80g fresh ginger, peeled and roughly chopped
- 1 whole chicken (about 2kg)
- 700g long grain rice, rinsed

Ginger sauce

- 500g ginger, peeled and chopped
- 20 garlic cloves, peeled
- 150ml chicken stock

Chicken soup

- 2 litres chicken soup
- 3 tbsp groundnut oil
- 6 shallots, peeled
- 10 garlic cloves, peeled
- 3 lemongrass stalks, roughly chopped
- 100g fresh ginger, peeled and roughly chopped

To serve

- 250g tofu, cut into pieces
- Finely chopped chives
- Cucumber slices, coriander leaves, julienned Chinese cabbage and carrot, and chilli and soy sauces

1 To make the ginger sauce, blend all the ingredients in a food processor until very fine, then sieve. Store in a jar in the fridge until ready to use.
2 For the soup, bring 4 litres of cold water to the boil in a stockpot. Add the shallots, garlic, lemongrass and ginger and return to the boil. Add the chicken with a small handful of sea salt and return to the boil for 5 minutes, then remove the pot from heat and set aside, covered, for 40 minutes to rest. Remove the chicken and transfer to a bowl of iced water. Leave for 30 minutes then drain into a colander.
3 To cook the rice, strain the chicken soup through a muslin-lined colander into a large bowl and set aside. Heat the oil in a large saucepan over a medium heat and fry the shallots, garlic, lemongrass and ginger till softened. Add the rice and cook for 5 minutes, stirring. Slowly ladle in about 2 litres of chicken soup, stirring till combined. Bring the rice to the boil, season with salt and white pepper. Reduce the heat to low and cook, covered, for 15 minutes, then remove the pot from the heat. Let the rice stand, covered, for 10 minutes. Keep warm until serving, then remove the shallots and other aromatics.
4 Meanwhile, reheat the remaining soup. Joint the cooked chicken with a sharp knife, removing the wings and legs. Halve the chicken lengthways and chop across in pieces. Take the meat off the bone. To serve, add the tofu to small soup bowls, pour the soup over the top and sprinkle with chopped chives. Place the chicken pieces on a large plate with a bowl of soup, a bowl of rice, the ginger sauce, chilli and soy sauces and a julienned vegetable salad garnish.

EDITOR'S FAVOURITE

DUCK RILLETTES

DUCK RILLETTES
Serves 2
- 2 duck legs
- 250g duck fat
- 2 garlic cloves, smashed
- 5 sprigs of thyme
- 50g pistachio nuts, chopped
- 50g sultanas, chopped
- 1 tsp red wine vinegar
- Sourdough toast, to serve

1 Preheat the oven to 150C/gas 2. Place the duck legs and fat in a roasting tray. Season, then tuck in the garlic and 3 thyme sprigs. Cover with foil and roast for 2 hours, or till the meat is falling off the bone. Remove from the oven. Once cool, discard the skin and shred the meat. Mix in the pistachios, sultanas, vinegar and remaining thyme leaves. Add enough cooking fat to bind the mixture, about 2 tablespoons. Season, then serve with as a snack or starter with crunchy toast.

SPRING CHICKEN & CITRUS STEW
This is a brilliant transitional dish. The stew element is warming, comforting and exactly what you want during the colder months, but there are also loads of flavours to remind you what's around the corner. Stirring in an avgolemono (lemon and egg) sauce is a traditional Greek method to freshen and lift stews.
Serves 4-6
- 3 tbsp olive oil
- 1 large chicken, portioned into legs, thighs, breasts and wings
- 6 garlic cloves, finely chopped
- 1 large onion, finely chopped
- 1 fennel bulb, finely chopped
- 1 small leek, trimmed, finely sliced
- A small bunch of parsley, stalks finely chopped, leaves reserved
- A small bunch of dill, stalks finely chopped, tops reserved
- A few stems of tarragon, stalks finely chopped, leaves reserved
- A large handful each of frozen peas, frozen broad beans and tinned cannellini beans
- A large handful of green olives, stoned
- Juice of 2 lemons
- 2 eggs, beaten
- 2 tbsp plain yoghurt
- Extra-virgin olive oil
- Parmesan cheese, for grating

1 Put a large casserole pan over a medium heat and add the olive oil. Season the chicken portions, then place in the casserole. Cook for about 10 minutes, turning, until the chicken is browned on all sides, then move to a plate. There should be a few tablespoons of fat left in the pan; if you have more, get rid of most of it before adding the garlic, onion, fennel, leek and herb stalks, and cooking till soft. 2 Put the chicken back in the pan, pour in 600ml water, then season with sea salt and black pepper. Cover with a lid, then cook over a medium-low heat for about an hour, until the chicken is tender and falling off the bone. Bring the mixture back up to a boil and stir in the peas, broad beans, cannellini beans and olives. When the frozen vegetables are done, add most of the herb leaves, reserving some to finish. 3 Remove the chicken from the stew and use 2 forks to pull the meat off the bones. Discard the bones, then return the meat to the pan. At this point, the stew will be delicious, but it's the next step that makes it amazing. 4 Beat the lemon juice and eggs well, then pour slowly into the stew. Don't stir it in too much; the egg mixture should add a gorgeous shine, not scramble. Stir in the yoghurt before ladling the stew into bowls. Drizzle a little extra-virgin olive oil over each bowl, grate over some parmesan, then sprinkle over the reserved herbs.

SPRING CHICKEN & CITRUS STEW

JAMIE
LOVES IT

FLYING STEAK SANDWICH

Good-quality pigeon is one of the most underrated meats you'll find. Feed this to your family or friends and they'll be forgiven for thinking it's the best steak sarnie they've ever had!

Serves 4-6

- 2-3 red onions, sliced
- Olive oil
- 4 sprigs of thyme, leaves picked
- 6 tbsp balsamic vinegar
- 1 large or 2 small ciabatta loaves
- 2 sprigs of rosemary, leaves picked and roughly chopped
- 8 pigeon breasts, skin on
- 1 bay leaf
- A knob of butter
- Extra-virgin olive oil
- English mustard, sprigs of watercress and 125g cottage cheese, to serve

1 An hour before you want to eat, preheat the oven to 180C/gas 4. Put the onions, a splash of olive oil, salt and pepper and half the thyme leaves into a roasting tray, then pop that in the oven. After 30 minutes, remove from the oven, stir well and add the balsamic vinegar. Cook for a few more minutes till they become sticky. Turn the heat off and pop the ciabatta loaf into the oven.
2 Heat a large nonstick pan on a high heat. Sprinkle the rosemary over the pigeon breasts, drizzle over some olive oil and season well. Toss the pigeon to coat in the flavoured oil. Once the pan is hot, add the pigeon, skin-side down, with the bay leaf, butter and remaining thyme leaves. Cook for 4-5 minutes, turning every minute for medium-rare meat. Pigeon is best served pink to medium. Anything over that and it will be a little tough. Slice on an angle, sprinkle over some salt and drizzle with olive oil.
3 Remove the bread and onions from the oven. Split the ciabatta, spread with mustard and add some watercress, the onions and the meat. Dot with cottage cheese, drizzle over any meat juices, replace the top of the bread and serve.

ROASTED PHEASANT WITH FENNEL

ROASTED PHEASANT WITH FENNEL

You could bone the pheasant yourself, but you may as well ask your butcher to do it for you - that's what he's there for!

Serves 2

- Olive oil
- 2 fennel bulbs, trimmed and diced into 2cm chunks
- A couple of thyme sprigs, leaves picked
- 1 pheasant, boned
- 2-3 garlic cloves, unpeeled
- 2-3 bay leaves
- 3-4 sprigs of rosemary
- Juice of ½ lemon
- A small pinch of dried chilli
- 2-3 tbsp mascarpone

1 Put a splash of oil in a high-sided pot over a medium heat. Add the fennel, season well, then pop on the lid. Stir every 5-10 minutes for 30-40 minutes, lowering the heat if the fennel colours too quickly, cooking it down till it's dark golden. Preheat the oven to 180C/gas 4.
2 About 15 minutes before the fennel is done, put a large ovenproof pan on a high heat. Rub the oil and thyme over the bird and season. Add a splash of oil to the pan. Slightly squash the garlic cloves with the back of a knife and add those to the pan with the bay leaves and the rosemary.
3 Put the bird in the pan skin-side down and push it down with tongs. Let the skin get crisp, and when it looks like the breast is about two-thirds cooked, use tongs to bend the breast up over the thighs so the thighs get most of the heat and the breast doesn't dry out. Cook for 3-4 minutes, then finish cooking in the oven, about 6-8 minutes. Once cooked, squeeze the lemon into the pan juices and swirl it, scraping up the bits from the bottom. Stir in the chilli and mascarpone to make a sauce. Taste and season the fennel, divide between plates and top with half a pheasant and the sauce.

PERFECT ROAST CHICKEN

PERFECT ROAST CHICKEN

Serves 4-6

- 1 chicken, about 1.6kg
- 2 garlic heads, sliced across the middle
- 5 large shallots, peeled
- A bunch of carrots, scrubbed
- 800g potatoes, peeled and quartered
- 1 lemon, quartered
- A handful of herbs such as bay leaves, tarragon and thyme
- 2 large knobs of butter
- 4 rashers of thick-cut streaky bacon
- Olive oil

1 Preheat the oven to 240C/gas 9. Remove the chicken from the fridge to get it to room temperature. Take a large baking tray and throw in the garlic, shallots, potatoes, a quarter of the lemon and the bay leaves.
2 Season the chicken generously inside and out, and stuff with a knob of butter, the remaining lemon and the herbs.

Wrap the chicken with the bacon rashers and top with the remaining butter. Season the vegetables in the tray and place the chicken on top. Drizzle the chicken and vegetables generously with olive oil and place in the hot oven. Immediately turn it down to 200C/gas 6 and cook the chicken for 80 minutes until the bacon is crisp and the chicken is cooked through. Check every half hour and add a splash of water to the vegetables if they look dry.
3 When your chicken is done, leave to rest for 10 minutes before carving and serving with the roast vegetables.

CRISPY DUCK SALAD WITH CROUTONS

Serves 4

- 1 duck
- Olive oil
- 1 tbsp five-spice powder
- 50g dried sour cherries

- A loaf of ciabatta, halved lengthways
- 2 garlic cloves
- 2 rosemary sprigs, leaves picked
- 6 clementines or blood oranges
- 4 tbsp balsamic vinegar
- 6 tbsp extra-virgin olive oil
- 1 red chicory
- 1 white chicory
- A bunch of watercress
- 4 mint sprigs, leaves picked

1 Preheat the oven to 160C/gas 2-3. Put the duck in a roasting tray and rub with oil and the five-spice. Season, and roast for 3½ hours. Soak the cherries in boiling water to rehydrate .
2 After 3½ hours, get the duck out of the oven to rest. Pour most of the fat from the tray into a clean jar (see note), leaving about 4 tablespoons in the tray. Crush the garlic into the tray, add the rosemary, then use the cut-side of the ciabatta halves to wipe up the flavoured fat. Put the bread in the tray, cut-side up and sprinkle over your rehydrated cherries. Put in the oven until golden and lovely.
3 Take 3 clementines and grate the zest of 2 into a small bowl, then squeeze in the juice of all 3. Mix in the balsamic vinegar and olive oil and season. Pull the leaves from the chicory and put them in a big bowl with the watercress.
4 Pull all the crispy skin off your duck. Remove the tray of bread, which should look like two giant croutons, from the oven. Cut each crouton in half and pull the duck skin apart over the top. Put the tray back in the oven to crisp a little more.
5 Meanwhile, shred the duck meat from the carcass. Spoon a few tablespoons of dressing over the meat to stop it drying out. Peel the remaining clementines and then slice them into rounds.
6 When the duck skin is really crisp and the croutons golden, remove from the oven. Add the shredded meat to the salad leaves and toss with enough of the dressing to coat. Scatter this over the croutons and the duck skin. Top with clementine slices and mint leaves.
Note Let the fat in the jar cool, then put the lid on and store in the fridge to use for lovely roast potatoes.

CROWD PLEASER

CRISPY DUCK SALAD WITH CROUTONS

SPANISH RABBIT STEW

SPANISH RABBIT STEW

There are a lot of gutsy rabbit stews made throughout Europe using regional wines. This one combines albariño, a white wine from Galicia, with paprika and peppers.

Serves 6-8

- 4 tbsp olive oil
- 2 small wild rabbits, jointed (if you're using farmed rabbits, you might only need 1 as they tend to be larger)
- 3 garlic cloves, sliced lengthways
- 12 small red onions, peeled and halved
- ½ tbsp sweet paprika
- 1 tbsp fresh rosemary leaves
- 750ml albariño
- 1 x 250-300g jar roasted red peppers, drained

1 Heat the olive oil in a large saucepan or cast-iron casserole over medium heat. Season the rabbit pieces and cook in batches, stirring occasionally, for about 5 minutes, or till browned. Transfer to a bowl and set aside.
2 Add the garlic and onions to the rabbit pan. Cook, stirring occasionally, till softened. Add the paprika and rosemary, season generously with sea salt and black pepper and stir well. Return the rabbit pieces to the pan, add the wine, cover with a folded piece of baking parchment, bring to the boil, then simmer for 1½-2 hours or until the rabbit is tender and the sauce has thickened, adding peppers for the final 15 minutes. If you like a thicker sauce, remove the rabbit pieces, then boil the sauce rapidly to reduce. If you wish, you can shred the meat then return it to the stew, so that you get both dark and light meat. Serve with crusty bread to mop up the sauces and a green salad.

COQ AU RIESLING

COQ AU RIESLING

We're all familiar with Burgundian coq au vin but each French region has a tradition of cooking poultry in its local wine. Many use white wine, like this delicious version from Alsace.

Serves 4-6

- 1.5kg chicken, cut into 8 pieces
- 750ml riesling
- 1 bouquet garni - celery, bay leaf and a sprig each of flat-leaf parsley and thyme, bound with kitchen string
- Olive oil
- 125g cubed streaky bacon
- 250g button mushrooms
- 12 small pickling onions, peeled
- 1 tbsp plain flour
- Finely chopped parsley and egg pasta or boiled potatoes, to serve

1 Marinate the chicken overnight in the wine and bouquet garni.
2 Heat the oil in a large frying pan. Remove the chicken from its marinade (reserving the wine and bouquet garni), pat dry and season. Add to the pan and brown on each side. Remove from the pan and set aside. Add another splash of oil to the pan, throw in the bacon and sauté for 5 minutes. Add the mushrooms and onions and sauté for another 5 minutes, or until softened.
3 Preheat the oven to 190C/gas 5. Transfer the bacon-mushroom mixture to a large, cast-iron casserole with a lid. Add the chicken, place on a medium heat, then add the flour and stir for a few minutes. Add the wine and bring to the boil. Season, add the bouquet garni and stir well. Cover, transfer to the oven and cook for 45 minutes or until the chicken is tender and the sauce is richer. Alternatively, simmer over a low heat for 45 minutes. If the chicken is cooked but the sauce needs thickening, remove the chicken and boil the sauce to reduce. Sprinkle with parsley and serve with the pasta or potatoes.

WORLD'S BEST TURKEY

WORLD'S BEST TURKEY

Take your bird out of the fridge a few hours before you cook it. You can truss its legs if you want, but it's not strictly necessary. The hot air will circulate around the legs and cook it evenly.

Serves 10-14

- 2-4 clementines, halved
- 2 large handfuls of fresh herbs such as rosemary, sage, bay and thyme
- A medium-sized turkey, about 6-8kg
- 2 large knobs of butter, or use our Christmas butter (page 163)
- 3 carrots, chopped
- 3 onions, peeled and thickly sliced
- 2 celery sticks, quartered
- 3 whole garlic heads, unpeeled
- Olive oil
- 4 spicy Italian sausages

1 Preheat the oven to full whack. Stuff the clementines and half the fresh herbs into the cavity of the turkey. Open up the neck cavity and stuff the butter under the skin, spreading it across the breasts. Pull the leaves off a large rosemary sprig and use it to spear through the loose skin around the bird's cavity to hold it together and keep it from shrinking back as the bird cooks.
2 In your largest roasting tray, make a vegetable trivet (the veg will create the gravy) by placing the carrots, onions, celery and garlic in the tray, scattering over the remaining herbs placing the turkey on top. Season the bird well, drizzle in olive oil and add a splash of water to the tray. Put in the oven and immediately turn down to 180C/gas 4.
3 As a rough guide, you want to cook the turkey for 35-40 minutes per kilo, so a 7kg turkey will want 4-4½ hours in the oven. Check your turkey every 30 minutes or so and keep it from drying out by basting it with the juices from the bottom of the pan. After 3½ hours, remove the foil so the skin turns golden.
4 Lift and angle the bird over the tray so the juices run out. Move to a platter, then cover it with a double layer of foil and 2 tea towels to keep it warm while it rests for at least 30 minutes.
5 Remove the veg from the tray and make a gravy with the remaining juices.

ONE TRAY WONDER

LEMON SURF 'N' TURF

LEMON SURF 'N' TURF

Sometimes it's nice to get your hands dirty and eat seriously sticky food. To keep it simple, everything is cooked in one pan. Don't forget the cold beers.

Serves 6

- 4 spicy Italian sausages
- 12 chicken wings
- 3 lemons, halved
- 1 truss of cherry tomatoes
- 18 large prawns, shell on
- A small bunch of thyme

Lemon marinade

- Zest of 1 lemon, juice of ½
- 4 tbsp olive oil
- 4 medium tomatoes
- 1 small onion, halved
- 8 garlic cloves
- 1 red chilli (you can remove the seeds if you don't like it too spicy)
- A small bunch each of basil and oregano

1 Preheat the oven to 180C/gas 4. Add all the marinade ingredients to a food processor and blitz until you have a thick paste, then put to one side.
2 Using a sharp knife, cut the sausages open and squeeze the meat filling into a bowl. Shape it into 12 meatballs with your hands (drizzle your hands with a little olive oil so the mixture doesn't stick). Put the meatballs into a large roasting tin with the chicken wings, lemon halves and cherry tomatoes.
3 Pour the marinade into the tin, then mix everything up so it gets a good coating. Put the tray in the oven and roast for 30 minutes. During cooking, give the tray a shake to move things around if they are colouring too much. Add the prawns, take the roasted lemons and squeeze over everything. Scatter over the thyme sprigs, then cook for another 10 minutes, until the marinade is sticky and the wings and prawns are cooked and golden. Take the tray to the table and serve with a big green salad and cold beers.

Saving the best till last

The evening's gone fabulously. The food you've spent ages preparing has gone down well, the wine you've chosen has been a big hit, and everyone's had a great time. So the last thing you want to do is spoil it all by not capping off the night with the best digestifs money can buy.

Which is where Johnnie Walker comes in. The brand has a noble pedigree – it's been a byword for excellence ever since young John Walker sold his first blended whisky from his Kilmarnock grocery in 1820. Johnnie Walker Gold Label was created 90 years ago to mark the centenary of this event. An 18-year-old deluxe blended scotch, it's a skilful fusion of 15 rare, aged whiskies from some of Scotland's most renowned distilleries.

The result is an exceptionally smooth taste, with malt, spices and almonds, and a lingering finish. For maximum impact, serve it straight from the freezer. Not only does this add a bit of theatre to the end of the meal, it also allows the whisky to gently release its honeyed flavours as it warms in the mouth. Serve with a few squares of dark chocolate for the perfect end to the evening.

If you really want to impress your guests, Johnnie Walker's ultra-premium expression, Blue Label, is a triumph of the master blender's art. Hand-crafted in limited quantities, each bottle draws upon the finest, rarest casks in the Johnnie Walker reserve. This gives it a velvety texture quite unparalled in other whiskies, while its flavour is a harmonious medley of hazelnuts, honey, rose petals, sherry and oranges.

As with all the finest things in life, Johnnie Walker Blue Label is best served simply. Just provide a glass of ice-cold highland spring water on the side so your guests can cleanse their palates beforehand, all the better to appreciate the ultra-premium nature of this wonderful whisky.

for the facts
drinkaware.co.uk

Meat

Things are about to get rare, charred, crisp and succulent. Indulge in slow-roast pork (page 111), host a fiesta with stuffed beef flank (page 119) and sink your teeth into steak & kidney pie (page 114). For something easy, rustle up beef & beetroot kebabs (page 116) or a comforting lamb hotpot (page 108)

GRILLED KOFTE

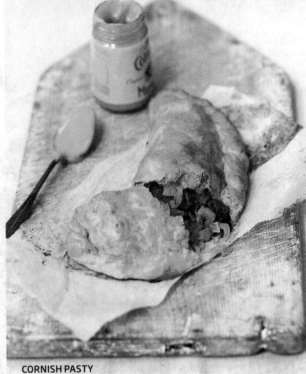

CORNISH PASTY

GRILLED KOFTE

Serves 4

- 500g minced lamb
- 1 small onion, grated
- 1 tsp each ground cumin and paprika
- ½ tsp ground coriander
- 3 tbsp finely chopped flat-leaf parsley
- Arab-style flatbread, enough for 4 people
- 500g baby spinach leaves, sautéed
- 150ml Greek-style plain yoghurt
- 1 tbsp za'atar (optional, see note)

Spicy tomato sauce

- 3 tbsp olive oil
- 200ml tomato passata
- ½ tbsp chilli powder

1 For the spicy tomato sauce, heat the oil in a saucepan over a medium heat. Stir in the passata and chilli powder and cook for 5 minutes. Lower the heat, season to taste and simmer for 20 minutes or till thickened.
2 For the kofte, mix the lamb, cumin, paprika, coriander and parsley, salt and pepper. Chill for at least 30 minutes before shaping the meat around 4 flat metal skewers. Make sure you don't put too much on each, as it won't cook all the way through and may fall off during cooking. Cook over a medium heat on a barbecue or hot griddle pan, turning, for 12–15 minutes or till cooked. At the end

of cooking, add the bread to the grill.
3 Top the bread with the spinach, then the yoghurt and the tomato sauce. Place the kofte on top, sprinkle with za'atar and serve immediately.
Note Za'atar is a Middle Eastern thyme-based herb blend available at speciality shops and big supermarkets.

CORNISH PASTY

This historic West Country pastry was originally eaten by poor families who could only afford cheap ingredients like swede, potato and onion – the meat came later.

Makes 6

- 300g maris piper potatoes, peeled
- ½ small swede, peeled
- 300g lean beef skirt or sirloin steak
- 2 medium onions, finely sliced
- White pepper
- A small bunch of flat-leaf parsley, chopped
- 25g butter
- 1 egg, beaten

Pastry

- 450g strong white plain flour
- 115g unsalted butter, chilled
- 115g lard, chilled

1 To make the pastry, mix the flour and a large pinch of sea salt in a bowl and coarsely grate in the very cold butter

and lard. Very gently rub the fat into the flour until it resembles breadcrumbs. Stir in 200ml cold water to bind the dough, which should be soft but not sticky. Knead together until the dough forms a ball, sprinkling with a little more flour if it feels too wet. Wrap in clingfilm and chill for 1 hour.
2 Meanwhile, prepare the filling. Cut the potatoes and swede into 5mm thick slices. Trim any gristle from the meat, then cut into small pieces, about 1cm in size, and add to the bowl. Add the onion and mix. Season with white pepper and sea salt and mix in the parsley.
3 Preheat the oven to 200C/gas 6. Divide the pastry into 6 portions. On a surface dusted with flour, shape each portion into a ball and roll out to about 24cm long and about 3mm thick.
4 Place a little of the meat mixture in the centre of the pastry, then put a small knob of butter on top. Brush the edge of the pastry with the beaten egg and fold the half nearest to you over the other side to seal. Press the edges together and crimp to seal.
5 Place the pasties on a baking tray lined with greaseproof paper and brush the tops with the beaten egg. Bake in the oven for about 35–40 minutes, until golden brown and firm. Cool a little before serving with English mustard and a nice pint of beer.

LAMB HOTPOT

LAMB HOTPOT
Serves 6
- 6 lamb chump chops
- Olive oil
- 2 celery sticks, chopped
- 1 onion, chopped
- 2 garlic cloves, chopped
- 1 potato, parboiled and sliced
- 1 x 400ml tin of cherry tomatoes
- 250ml tomato passata
- 1 glass of dry white wine

1 Season the lamb. Place a cast-iron casserole dish over a medium heat, add a little olive oil and brown the meat. Remove it from the pan and transfer to a dish. Add the celery, onion and garlic to the pan and sauté for 5 minutes, or till they have softened . Add the potatoes and season, then add the tin of cherry tomatoes, tomato passata and white wine. Stir well, then turn up the heat and bring to the boil. Lower the heat and simmer for 40 minutes, or until the lamb is tender, the potatoes are cooked and the sauce has thickened.

Roll up, roll up

Meatballs are loved by kids and adults alike and are so easy to make – add salt, pepper and other flavourings to mince, then roll and fry till cooked. For an Italian version, combine minced veal and pork with fennel seeds, sage and parmesan. For a Swedish classic, mix beef and pork mince with chopped dill - cook in a sauce made from stock, cream and currant jam. Make Moroccan-style meatballs of lamb mince, currants, pine nuts, ground cumin and chopped coriander. Or try a version with lamb, finely chopped leeks and dried mint. For a Latin vibe, mix minced pork with smoked paprika, dry sherry, parsley and puréed roasted peppers. If you like it hot, mix beef mince with roasted garlic cloves, chopped red chilli, chilli flakes, chopped red onion and thyme.

PORK & SPINACH MEATBALLS
Serves 4
- 3 large handfuls of spinach
- 500g pork mince
- 1 egg, beaten
- ½ tsp ground nutmeg
- Zest of 1 lemon
- 4 handfuls of breadcrumbs
- 1 garlic clove, sliced
- Olive oil
- Tomato pasta sauce (or chopped tomatoes), chopped herbs and grated parmesan, to serve

1 Steam the spinach, then allow to cool. Squeeze out the liquid and roughly chop. In a bowl, mix the pork mince with the egg, nutmeg, lemon zest, spinach and breadcrumbs. Season well, and shape into small balls.
2 Fry in with the garlic in a little olive oil for 7-8 minutes, until cooked through. Top with a hot tomato sauce, some chopped herbs and parmesan. Serve with rice, bread or potatoes. These meatballs are also great with pasta.

KIDS
LOVE IT

SLOW-ROAST PORK WITH SALSA ROSSA

CROWD PLEASER

SLOW-ROAST PORK WITH SALSA ROSSA

By starting off the pork at a high heat and then turning it down, you'll get both crackling and soft, rich meat. How long the pork takes depends on the size of the shoulder. If you want to serve this for dinner, you'll need to get it started first thing in the morning.
Serves 20

- 4 tbsp fennel seeds
- 1 tbsp coriander seeds
- 2 tbsp sea salt
- 2 fennel bulbs, trimmed and chopped
- 4 medium carrots, roughly chopped
- 3 onions, roughly chopped
- 1 garlic bulb, cloves unpeeled but smashed
- A bunch of thyme
- 1 whole shoulder of pork, skin scored - ask your butcher to do this
- Olive oil
- Bread rolls, rocket leaves and dijon mustard, to serve

Salsa rossa
- Olive oil
- 2 scotch bonnet peppers, deseeded and chopped
- 4 red chillies, deseeded and chopped
- 1 red onion, quartered
- 3 red peppers, deseeded
- 2 quinces or pears, cored and chopped
- 2 x 400g tins plum tomatoes
- 2 bay leaves
- 1 cinnamon stick
- 1 tbsp dried oregano
- Red wine vinegar
- 4 handfuls of chopped herbs (use whichever you have available)

1 Preheat the oven to maximum. Place the fennel seeds, coriander seeds and salt in a food processor and whizz until fine. Put the chopped vegetables, garlic and thyme into a large roasting tray. Pat the pork shoulder dry and rub it all over with the fennel mix, then sit it on top of the vegetables in the tray. Put the pork in the oven for 20-30 minutes, until it starts to colour, then turn your oven down to 120C/gas ½ and cook the pork slowly for 8-12 hours, until the meat is soft and sticky and you can pull it apart easily with a fork.
2 When your pork is nearly ready, start your salsa. Put the chillies, onion and red pepper into a food processor and whizz until finely chopped. Over a medium heat, add a little oil to a large frying pan, and sweat the onion-pepper mixture till soft and sweet, about 15-20 minutes. Add the quince or pear to the pan and cook for 20 minutes. Add the tomatoes, bay leaves, cinnamon and oregano and season well with sea salt and freshly ground black pepper. Turn down the heat and leave to simmer for 40 minutes, until the sauce is dense and syrupy. Finish it off with a good splash of red wine vinegar, some more seasoning and a good sprinkle of the chopped herbs.
3 Once your pork is meltingly soft, take it out the oven. Remove the crackling and cover the meat in tin foil to keep warm while you do the finishing touches. Break the crackling up into pieces. Shred some of the pork and move the whole lot onto a big board, with some salad some toasted ciabatta, bowls of simply dressed rocket, mustard and the salsa.

LAMB'S LIVER WITH PEAS & BEANS

LAMB'S LIVER WITH PEAS & BEANS

Serves 2
- 6 medium slices of lamb's livers
- Seasoned plain flour
- 2 garlic cloves, sliced
- 2 tsp olive oil
- 2 large handfuls each of fresh peas and broad beans, podded
- A knob of butter
- Red wine vinegar
- A large pinch of chopped parsley
- Mint leaves, to serve

1 Dust the livers in seasoned plain flour. Place a frying pan on a medium-high heat, fry the garlic with oil for a minute - don't let it colour - then add the liver. Cook, turning, for 3-4 minutes, until crisp. Remove and keep warm. Add the peas and beans, butter, a dash of vinegar and the parsley and cook till tender. Season and return the liver to the pan to heat, then finish with mint.

SPRING LAMB WITH WHITE WINE & LEEKS

Sausage roles

Good-quality bangers are available widely and are brilliant for quick fixes. Grilled chorizo makes the best sausage sandwich, just add fried onions and rocket. Slice sausages and courgettes and thread onto a skewer with baby tomatoes, then grill. Make a cassoulet by placing sausages in casserole with chicken drumsticks, white beans, thyme, a splash of wine and baking till everything is cooked. For scotch eggs, press sausage meat around boiled eggs, crumb them and carefully deep-fry. Remove sausage meat from the skins, press into patties, season, fry then serve with eggs. Or fry the meat in a hot pan, breaking up with a spoon, till crunchy, then sprinkle over a salad. For toad in the hole, brown sausages, put in a tray, pour over yorkshire pudding batter and put in a very hot oven till risen and cooked.

KIDS LOVE IT

STICKY SAUSAGES

SPRING LAMB WITH WHITE WINE & LEEKS

Slow and low – that's the best way to cook lamb. This is an easy take on the Sunday roast – these casseroled shanks take just 10 minutes to get going, then you leave them be. Using white wine instead of the more usual red lends the dish lighter, brighter flavour suitable for springtime. Lovely with roast potatoes and our mint and pistachio sauce (page 160).
Serves 8
- Olive oil
- 2 large leeks, trimmed and chopped
- 2 celery sticks, chopped
- 1 tsp each cumin and caraway seeds
- 1 tbsp smoked paprika
- A few sprigs of mint, leaves picked and finely chopped
- 8 lamb shanks
- A bottle of good-quality white wine
- 1 garlic head, broken into cloves, unpeeled
- 1 dried red chilli, crumbled
- A small bunch of thyme

1 Get your largest saucepan with a lid on a medium heat. Add a good splash of oil and sauté the leeks and celery for 10 minutes, until they're soft.
2 Bash the caraway and cumin seeds in a pestle and mortar, then add the paprika, mint, sea salt and pepper and a tiny splash of oil. Mix it up well, then rub over the shanks before placing snugly in the pan with the leeks and celery.
3 Pour over the wine, throw in the garlic cloves, the chilli and the sprigs of thyme. The shanks should be almost covered – if they aren't, top up with water or stock. Bring the liquid to a simmer, then cover and cook gently for 2½–3 hours, until the meat is soft and succulent and practically falling off the bone. If there's a lot of liquid left, remove the lid and simmer for the last half-hour, or till the sauce thickens.

STICKY SAUSAGES
These are really easy to make for a barbecue or casual party.
Serves 4
- 3 tbsp of maple syrup
- Olive oil
- A small bunch of rosemary
- 18 mini sausages or 12 chipolatas
- Dijon mustard, to serve

1 In a bowl, combine the maple syrup with a good splash of olive oil and a pinch of sea salt and freshly ground pepper. If you're using mini sausages, you can remove the rosemary leaves and use the woody stems as skewers. Otherwise, use the rosemary as a brush to spread the glaze onto sausages.
2 Heat a large saucepan over medium heat and drizzle with olive oil. Fry the sausages, in batches if necessary, until they are sticky and cooked through. Glaze with the leftover syrup and serve with mustard and jacket potatoes.

STEAK & KIDNEY PIE

BEEF DAUBE

The meat needs to absorb all the aromatic flavours overnight, so get it marinating before you go to bed. It then needs 4-5 hours to cook so would be an ideal late lunch or dinner.
Serves 10

- 3 large onions, 2 thinly sliced
- 2kg beef chuck, cut into 8-10cm pieces
- 2 large carrots, thickly sliced
- 6 garlic cloves, sliced
- 2 celery sticks, including leaves, coarsely chopped
- 1 x 8cm strip dried or fresh orange peel
- 1 bouquet garni – celery, bay leaf and a sprig each of thyme and flat-leaf parsley, bound with kitchen string
- 1 cinnamon stick
- 10 black peppercorns, crushed
- 5 juniper berries, crushed
- 5 cloves
- 750ml dry red wine
- 125ml red wine vinegar
- 4 tbsp plain flour, for dusting
- 100ml extra-virgin olive oil
- 300g bacon or pancetta, cut into batons
- 80g black olives
- Macaroni or rigatoni and grated parmesan, to serve

STEAK & KIDNEY PIE

Recipe by Trevor Oliver & Justin Grieg, The Cricketers, Clavering
A proper British classic, from the pub owned by Jamie's dad.
Serves 6

- 250g self-raising flour
- 125g suet
- 20g butter
- Olive oil
- 400g lean beef, cubed
- 100g kidneys, chopped
- 1 large onion, roughly chopped
- 1 tbsp tomato purée
- 1 tbsp plain flour
- ½ tbsp worcestershire sauce
- 570ml beef stock
- 2 fresh bay leaves

1 On a floured surface, combine the flour and suet with 150ml water and a pinch of salt until you have a dough. Don't overwork the dough.
2 Heat the butter and a splash of olive oil in a saucepan over a medium heat and sauté the beef, then the kidneys, for 3-5 minutes each, until browned. Transfer to a bowl with a slotted spoon.
3 Sauté the onions for 3-5 minutes, until softened. Return the beef and kidneys to the saucepan. Add the tomato purée and the flour and cook for 5-7 minutes, stirring. Add the worcestershire sauce, stock and bay leaves and bring to the boil. Turn down the heat to low and simmer, stirring occasionally, for 1½-2 hours or until the meat is tender and the sauce has thickened. Season to taste.
4 Roll out the pastry to a thickness of 2-3mm, then place in 10cm/300ml metal moulds, making sure the pastry comes up to the top. Add the filling. Cover with more pastry, cutting off the excess edges. Bake at 190C/gas 5 for 25 minutes until the pastry has puffed up and is golden. Serve with mashed potato, rich beef gravy and a pint of ale.

1 Put the sliced onions in a bowl with the beef, carrot, garlic, celery, orange peel, bouquet garni and spices. Season, then add the wine and vinegar. Cover and leave to marinate in the fridge overnight.
2 In the morning, remove beef from the marinade (reserving the marinade), pat dry with kitchen paper and dust with flour. Heat half the oil in a large casserole dish. Brown the meat in batches, then transfer to a bowl and set aside.
3 Chop the remaining onion and add to the pan with the bacon. Sauté on a medium heat for 5-7 minutes, or until soft. Add the meat and reserved marinade to the pan, along with enough water to cover the meat and vegetables. Cover with a folded piece of baking parchment. Bring to the boil over a low-medium heat, then turn down the heat to very low and simmer until the sauce reduces and thickens and the meat is tender (4-5 hours). Stir in the olives and season. Serve with pasta and salad and sprinkle over parmesan.

BEEF DAUBE

BEEF & BEETROOT KEBABS

STEAK WITH OLIVE & ALMOND PICADA

Used in Catalan cuisine, a picada is a kind of paste made from almonds, bread and other flavourings. It's often used towards the end of cooking to thicken sauces and stews, though here it's served as a complement to steak.

Serves 4

- 12 spring onions, bases trimmed but with the green tops left on
- 4 x 200g large sirloin steaks
- 1 tbsp dried oregano
- 1 tbsp olive oil

Green olive & almond picada
- 100g green olives, stoned
- 100g blanched almonds
- A handful of breadcrumbs
- Zest of 1 lemon
- 1 tbsp extra-virgin olive oil

Tomato, red onion & green olive salad
- 2 large tomatoes, cut into wedges
- 1 red onion, peeled and thinly sliced
- 20 green olives, stones in
- 3 tbsp olive oil
- 1 tbsp sherry vinegar

1 Combine all the picada ingredients in a food processor. Whizz to a rough paste and put aside. In a large bowl, toss the salad ingredients and set aside.
2 When you're almost ready to eat, sprinkle the onions and steak with salt, pepper, oregano and olive oil. Grill on a medium-hot barbecue or griddle pan, turning once, until the steak and onions are cooked to your liking. Let the steaks rest briefly, then serve with the picada sprinkled on top and salad on the side.

BEEF & BEETROOT KEBABS

Serves 4
- A handful of basil leaves
- ½ a red chilli
- 2 garlic cloves
- Olive oil
- 500g beef, cut in 2cm pieces
- 300g baby beetroots

1 Bash the basil in a mortar with the chilli, garlic, sea salt and black pepper and a good splash of oil. Add to a bowl with the beef and mix well, then place in the fridge for 30 minutes.
2 Preheat the oven to 200C/gas 6 and soak some wooden skewers in water. Boil the beetroot in salted water for 10 minutes. Drain, drizzle over olive oil, season and roast for 25 minutes, till tender. Thread the beef and beetroot onto the skewers. Grill or barbecue for 5 minutes, until the beef is cooked. Sprinkle with extra chilli and basil leaves.

15
MINUTE
MEAL

STEAK WITH OLIVE & ALMOND PICADA

EDITOR'S FAVOURITE

STUFFED BEEF FLANK WITH SPICY SALSA

STUFFED BEEF FLANK WITH SPICY SALSA

Serves 6

- 1-1.2kg piece of beef flank, butterflied
- 100g sliced ham
- 100g swiss chard
- 1 x 300g jar of red peppers, drained and roughly chopped
- 1 red onion, thinly sliced
- 3 hard-boiled eggs, quartered
- 3 tbsp breadcrumbs
- 1 tbsp finely chopped flat-leaf parsley
- ½ tbsp dried oregano
- ½ tbsp paprika
- Olive oil

Spicy tomato & onion salsa

- 1 red onion, finely chopped
- 1 tbsp chopped parsley
- 1 tbsp paprika
- 6 tbsp olive oil
- 3 tbsp sherry vinegar
- 120ml Spanish tomato frito (see note)

1 Lay the ham slices and swiss chard over the beef. Top with the peppers, onions, eggs, breadcrumbs, herbs and spices. Roll up and tie tightly with kitchen string. Brown in a pan with some olive oil.
2 Preheat the oven to 200C/gas 6. Put the meat in a roasting tin and cover with water. Cover the tray with foil and put in the oven for 45–60 minutes, or till tender.
3 Remove from the oven, move to a plate and cover with clingfilm. Place in the fridge with a plate on top to weigh the meat down. Cool completely.
4 Meanwhile, mix the salsa ingredients in a bowl. Season, and put aside.
5 When you're ready to eat, thickly slice the beef, then serve with some of the salsa drizzled over and on the side.
Note Spanish tomato frito is a thin sauce made with fried tomatoes. It is available ready-made, from speciality shops. If you can't find it substitute with passata thinned with a little water.

PORK ADOBO & PEPPER SALAD

PORK ADOBO & PEPPER SALAD

Serves 6

- 1-1.2kg pork loin

Marinade

- 4 garlic cloves, peeled
- 1 tbsp dried oregano
- A pinch of saffron threads
- 1 tbsp paprika
- 2 tbsp olive oil
- 2 tbsp red wine vinegar

Mixed pepper salad

- 6 long green peppers
- 4 small pimientos de padrón (optional)
- 1 x 220g jar of piquillo peppers, drained
- 3 garlic cloves, finely sliced
- 1 white onion, finely sliced
- 6 tbsp olive oil
- 2 tbsp red wine vinegar
- A few sprigs of fresh basil

1 With a pestle and mortar, pound the garlic, oregano, saffron and paprika together until you get a smooth paste. Add the olive oil and vinegar and mix to combine. Put the pork in a bowl and rub the marinade all over it. Cover and refrigerate overnight.
2 Blacken the peppers and pimientos under a hot grill, allow to cool, then peel and deseed. Shred the flesh and add it to a bowl, along with the garlic and onion. Pour over the olive oil and red vinegar. Toss together and tear over the basil.
3 When you're ready to eat, remove the pork loin from the fridge and cut into thick, 5cm steaks. Cook over a medium heat on a barbecue or griddle pan for 7–8 minutes on each side, until tender and cooked through to your liking. Serve with the pepper salad.

BEEF & BARLEY STEW

BEEF & BARLEY STEW

Serves 4

- 2 tbsp olive oil
- 1 onion, roughly chopped
- 1 garlic clove, roughly chopped
- 1 carrot, roughly chopped
- 1 leek, roughly chopped
- 2 celery sticks, roughly chopped
- 1 tbsp chopped parsley leaves and stems
- 250g butternut squash, cubed
- 450g diced beef shin
- 100g pearl barley
- 1.5 litres beef stock

1 Heat the olive oil in a large pan over a medium heat. Sauté the vegetables and parsley until soft.
2 Season the beef shin, add to the pan and continue cooking until browned. Stir through the pearl barley, and pour over the beef stock. Simmer for 90 minutes, or until the meat is tender.

SPICY VEAL CHOPS

Serves 2

- 2 x 350g veal chops
- 1 tbsp thyme leaves
- 1 garlic clove, roughly chopped
- 1 shallot, roughly chopped
- 1 tbsp roughly chopped parsley, leaves only
- 1 habanero chilli, finely chopped
- Juice of ½ lemon
- 2 tbsp olive oil

Caramelised onions

- 1 tbsp butter
- 1 tbsp olive oil
- 1 large white onion, finely sliced
- 1 tbsp brown sugar

1 Place the chops in a large bowl with the other ingredients. Mix well, then set aside to marinate. Meanwhile, place a large frying pan on a low heat and add the butter and olive oil. When the butter has melted, throw in the onions and fry for a couple of minutes before stirring in the sugar. Cook for 10 minutes, or till the onions are soft and golden brown.
2 Brush the marinade off the chops and cook them on a hot griddle pan or frying pan for 3-4 minutes each side, or to your liking. Leave to rest while you heat the marinade in the pan. Spoon over the marinade and serve with the onions.

Slow & steady

Stew is an undemanding yet rewarding supper. Once it's simmering you can leave it until you're ready to eat. Cheaper cuts of meat are great as they get more tender the longer they cook. Brown braising steak with onions, add carrots and parsnips, cover with Guinness and cook for 2 hours. Cover leftovers with shortcrust pastry to make a pie. Get Moroccan by browning chicken thighs in a casserole dish and throw in some onions, paprika, preserved lemon, green olives and stock. Wrap leftovers in filo parcels. For a pork and cider stew, cook pork shoulder with celery and a cinnamon stick then cover with cider. To make a Greek-inspired stew, brown lamb meat with garlic, dried oregano and mint, then simmer with tinned tomatoes and finish with a squeeze of lemon.

JAMIE'S FAVOURITE

Top escalopes

Beating meat – such as beef or pork steaks, or chicken breast – with a rolling pin helps tenderise it, and makes it thinner, so it cooks quickly. Perfect coated with crumbs and fried for midweek meals! Use the coating from this escalope recipe to put on flattened chicken breasts, or even thin fish fillets. You can give an extra dimension of flavour by adding paprika to the seasoned flour, or by mixing some grated parmesan into the breadcrumbs, or even grating in some lemon zest. For an easy saltimbocca, press 2 sage leaves and a thin slice of pancetta on to a veal escalope, then beat with a rolling pin to help it stick before pan-frying. Likewise, you could press thin slices of aubergine and provolone cheese to a beaten pork steak, before crumbing and frying, while prosciutto works well with chicken.

QUICK VEAL ESCALOPES

BLACK & BLUSHING BEEF FILLET

This is a really delicious way of barbecuing your beef. It's going to look really dark and burnt on the outside, but it'll be perfect inside .
Serves 4

- 600–700g piece of fillet steak
- 2 heaped tsp French mustard
- 8–10 tbsp worcestershire sauce, plus extra for drizzling
- Extra-virgin olive oil
- 2 sprigs of rosemary, leaves chopped
- A large knob of cold butter
- Thyme flowers, to serve (optional)

1 The day (or at least a few hours) before cooking, put all the ingredients into a large sandwich bag. Squeeze out the air, then massage all the flavours into the meat and leave to rest in the fridge. About 1½ hours before you're ready to cook, remove the beef from the fridge to allow it to come up slowly to room temperature. Preheat your barbecue or griddle pan. **2** Take the fillet out the bag and pat it dry with kitchen paper. Roll it in olive oil and put it in the hottest part of the barbecue or the centre of the griddle pan. Rub it with the cold butter as you cook it for about 8-10 minutes, turning every minute. Once it looks good and dark, move the fillet to a cooler part of the barbecue or turn down the temperature of your hob and finish cooking to your liking. Another 4-5 minutes, turning every minute, should give you medium meat. If you like it medium-rare, cook it for a shorter time, or longer for well-done. **3** When it's done, put it on a platter, rub it again with butter, then drizzle over more worcestershire sauce, olive oil, and thyme flowers, if you have them. **4** Let the meat rest for a few minutes before slicing. Season again, and serve with the meat juices.

QUICK VEAL ESCALOPES

Serves 2

- 1–2 garlic cloves, sliced
- Olive oil
- A pinch of chilli powder
- 1 x 400g tin cherry tomatoes
- 2 veal escalopes
- 2 tbsp seasoned flour
- 1 egg, beaten
- 2 large handfuls fresh breadcrumbs
- Lightly toasted pine nuts, basil and parmesan, to serve

1 In a small pan, fry the garlic and chilli in a little oil. Once the garlic has taken on a little colour, add the tomatoes. Season and cook until the veal is done. **2** Dip the veal first in the flour, then the egg and lastly in the breadcrumbs. In a frying pan, fry the veal in olive oil for 3-4 minutes on each side, till cooked. Serve with the tomato sauce, toasted pine nuts, basil and parmesan.

Desserts

If proof of the pudding is in the eating, what are you waiting for? We dare you to resist our comforting stone-fruit and ginger crumble (page 126) or the epic brownie gâteau (page 130). For something cold, how about rich treacle ice cream (page 130) or a fresh and zesty plum sorbet (page 141). If you're out to impress, chocolate and sea salt tart (page 131) is a winner

CHOCOLATE SORBET

WINTER PUDDING BOMBE

CHOCOLATE SORBET

Serves 6-8

- 75g good-quality cocoa powder
- 300g golden caster sugar
- 1 vanilla pod, split, seeds scraped
- 300g dark chocolate (70% cocoa solids), broken into small pieces

1 Pour 750ml water into a saucepan with the cocoa, sugar and the vanilla pod and seeds. Bring to the boil, whisking constantly, then remove from the heat. Add the chocolate and a pinch of salt and leave for a minute, then whisk until the chocolate has melted and you have a glossy mixture. Cool, then transfer to an ice-cream maker and freeze. Alternatively, pour into a shallow tray and place in the freezer, removing every hour or two to break up the ice crystals with a fork, until frozen.

WINTER PUDDING BOMBE

This is a cross between a summer pudding and an arctic roll, so it's seriously retro. It's an assembly job, so everybody can make this, even those who say they can't cook.

Serves 10

- 2 x 500ml tubs of good vanilla ice cream
- About ½ standard panettone
- 125ml vin santo
- 2-3 tbsp good raspberry jam
- A handful of pistachios, shelled
- 1-2 handfuls of tinned sour cherries, drained
- 2-3 glacé clementines (or other glacé fruit), thinly sliced
- 2 clementines, 1 peeled and sliced into rounds
- 200g dark chocolate (70% cocoa solids), bashed

1 Get your ice cream out of the freezer so it can soften a little while you get things ready. Line a 2-litre bowl with 3 sheets of clingfilm. Use a serrated knife to slice a few rounds (four 2cm-thick slices should be enough) off your panettone, then slice them in half. Arrange 6 of the slices in a single layer over the sides and bottom of the bowl; push them down if they overlap. Drizzle vin santo around the pannettone so it soaks in, then spread over the jam.
2 Add 1 tub of ice cream to the bowl and use a spoon to spread it around in a thick layer. Sprinkle over the pistachios, glacé fruit and cherries, layer the clementine slices on top, then spread over the other tub of ice cream. Put the other slices of panettone on top of the ice cream, drizzle over more vin santo, then cover tightly with clingfilm. Put a plate on top to press it down, then freeze overnight, or longer.
3 When you're ready to serve, put the chocolate in a bowl over a pan with a little water in it on a really low heat. Leave it to melt while you unwrap your amazing bombe and carefully turn it onto a beautiful serving dish. Add grated clementine zest to the melted chocolate, then pour it over the top so it oozes down and looks delicious.

STONE-FRUIT & GINGER CRUMBLE

STONE-FRUIT & GINGER CRUMBLE
Serves 6

- 1kg stone fruit - peaches, nectarine, red or yellow plums - trimmed, stoned and sliced into large chunks
- 500g strawberries, hulled
- 150g soft brown sugar
- Zest and juice of 1 orange
- 4 sprigs of lemon verbena (optional)
- 100g plain flour
- 100g butter
- 100g oats
- 3 pieces of stem ginger, chopped

1 Preheat your oven to 180C/gas 4. Put the fruit, orange zest and juice and the lemon verbena (if you have it) into a roasting tray, along with 50g sugar. Put in the oven and roast for 20 minutes until the fruit is syrupy and softened.
2 Meanwhile, for your crumble topping, use your fingers to lightly rub the flour into the butter until the mixture resembles fine breadcrumbs. Stir in the oats, the rest of the sugar and the ginger. (You can make the topping in a food processor. Just whack in the flour, butter, sugar and ginger and whizz up. Add the oats for the last 10 seconds.) Generously sprinkle the topping over the fruit, put back in the oven and bake for 40-45 minutes, or until the fruit is bubbling up and the topping is golden and crunchy. Serve with vanilla ice cream or rich Greek yoghurt.

CHERRY ICE CREAM & CHERRY-TARRAGON COULIS
Serves 8

- 300ml single cream
- 1 vanilla pod, split, seeds scraped
- 4 egg yolks
- 125g caster sugar, plus 2 tbsp extra
- 300ml double cream
- 250g cherries, stoned
- 45ml kirsch
- 100g amaretti biscuits, crumbled

Cherry-tarragon coulis
- 100g cherries, stoned
- 1 tbsp caster sugar
- A few tarragon leaves
- Juice of ½ lime

1 Heat the cream and vanilla seeds in a pan over a medium heat till the cream starts to steam. Set aside to infuse.
2 Meanwhile, whisk the egg yolks with the sugar till thick and pale. Pour the vanilla cream over the egg mixture and whisk till smooth. Pour back into the pan, stirring constantly with a wooden spoon over a low heat until it has thickened. You can test that it is done by running your finger across the back of the spoon – it should leave a broad line. Remove from the heat and let it cool to room temperature. Chill for 30 minutes, then stir in the double cream; chill again.
3 Meanwhile, cook the cherries with the kirsch and the 2 tablespoons of caster sugar until softened. Purée in a food processor or with a hand-held blender. Chill until cool, then stir into the chilled cream mixture.
4 Pour this mixture into an ice-cream maker and churn. When it has thickened, stir in the amaretti chunks. Transfer to a plastic container and freeze till needed.
5 For the coulis, heat the cherries, sugar and tarragon in 100ml water, then simmer for 10 minutes or so, until the cherries have softened. Leave to cool. Add the lime juice and purée in a food processor or with a hand-held blender.
6 Allow the ice cream to soften slightly before drizzling with the coulis, either in a cone or a bowl.

GROWN-UP
TREAT

CHERRY ICE CREAM & CHERRY-TARRAGON COULIS

CROWD PLEASER

CHERRY BROWNIES

Cherry amour

Cherries are a highlight of summer. Add stoned cherries and lemon zest strips to a sugar syrup and simmer for 5 minutes, then spoon over french toast and top with ice cream. Make a cherry mess by stirring chopped ones through whipped cream and crushed meringue. Drop a handful or two of the fruit into a bottle of brandy and a month later, make a cocktail with a little brandy, topped up with champagne and throw in a boozy cherry. For a jelly, blitz stoned cherries with apple juice, gently heat and add gelatine according to packet instructions and chill in the fridge till set, then eat with whipped cream. Or just pick them up by the stalk, dip into melted dark chocolate and leave to set in the fridge.

CHERRY COBBLER

CHERRY BROWNIES

Makes 16 squares
- 130g butter
- 150g dark chocolate (70%-cocoa)
- 55g cherries, stoned, roughly chopped
- 55g roasted pecans, roughly chopped
- 225g caster sugar
- 55g cocoa powder
- 75g plain flour
- ¾ tsp baking powder
- 3 eggs, beaten
- 50g milk or dark chocolate, roughly chopped (optional)

1 Preheat the oven to 180C/gas 4. Line a 20cm square baking tin (or equivalent) with baking parchment.
2 Melt the butter and the 150g chocolate in a bowl over a saucepan of simmering water (don't let the bowl touch the water). Stir in the cherries and nuts, then take off the heat.
3 In another bowl, add the sugar, then sift in the cocoa powder, flour and

baking powder. Add to the chocolate mixture and stir until well combined. Mix in the eggs. If using, stir through the chopped chocolate.
4 Transfer the mixture to the tin, then bake in the oven for 15–20 minutes. You want them a little gooey in the middle. Remove from the oven and cool in the tray, before cutting into squares.

CHERRY COBBLER

Cobblers are traditional English fruit pies with a scone-like topping. The overall affect looks a little bit like a cobbled street, hence the name.
Serves 6
- 600g cherries, stoned
- A good squeeze of lime juice
- 225g caster sugar, plus a pinch or two
- 110g self-raising flour
- 1 tsp baking powder
- 40g butter, chilled and diced
- 1 egg yolk

- 50ml buttermilk
- A small handful of flaked almonds

1 Preheat the oven to 180C/gas 4. Mix the cherries, lime juice and 175g caster sugar in the base of a 24cm pie dish.
2 To make the cobbler topping, beat the egg yolk with the buttermilk. In another bowl, sieve together the flour, baking powder and 50g of the sugar. Add the butter and, using your fingertips, rub the butter into the flour until the mixture resembles breadcrumbs. Pour in the egg mixture, then combine until the ingredients are mixed and you have a sticky dough.
3 Drop walnut-sized pieces of the dough onto the surface of the fruit, leaving gaps between for your scones to expand into. Sprinkle over the flaked almonds and a pinch or two of sugar. Place the pie dish into the oven and bake for 25 minutes until the scones are golden brown and the fruit is bubbling.

TREACLE ICE CREAM

simmering water. Meanwhile, sift the flour, baking powder and cocoa. If using whole almonds, whizz them up in a food processor until they are fine.

3 Once the chocolate mixture has melted, remove from the heat. Whisk the egg whites until stiff, add sugar and whisk lightly again. Set aside. Add the chocolate mixture to the yolks, mixing firmly but gently. Fold this mixture into the egg whites. Take care not to be too heavy-handed and stop mixing as the last of the white disappears. Fold in the flour and almonds. Divide between the cake tins and bake for 25-30 minutes. The cake should be firm and cooked on the outside but still quite soft inside.

4 To make the honey-roasted almonds, spread the almonds out on a tray, drizzle over the honey and mix with your hands so they are roughly covered. Once the brownie cake has baked, remove it from the oven and pop the honey-almond mixture in for 5-10 minutes, until golden.

5 Allow the cake to cool completely before removing from the tins. Once the almonds are done, loosen them from the tray, and break or bash up into small praline pieces. Allow to cool.

6 Once the cake has cooled, make the ganache icing. Heat the cream in a saucepan on a low heat. Just before boiling point, drop in the chocolate and remove from the heat. Stir until the chocolate is smooth and glossy.

7 Saving the prettiest cake for the top, place the other layer on a plate or a cake stand. They will still be a little soft in the middle so handle with care. Spread the bottom layer with about one-third of the ganache icing then place the other cake on top. Using the back of a spoon to create peaks and troughs, spread the rest of the icing on top of the cake. Sprinkle over the honeyed almonds and serve with crème fraîche or ice cream.

TREACLE ICE CREAM
Serves 4
- 2 eggs
- 1 egg yolk
- 450ml double cream
- 125ml treacle (or to taste)

1 To make this rich ice cream, whisk the eggs and egg yolk together until thick and pale. Mix in the cream and treacle. Churn in an ice-cream maker according to manufacturer's instructions. Serve with sponge cake or baked apples.

EPIC BROWNIE GATEAU

This is not a cake to be taken lightly, or even every day. It's a dark, smudgy and dense. It can be made the day before you serve it – make the ganache icing and assemble the cake on the day.
Serves 12-20
- 400g unsalted butter

- 400g 70%-cocoa chocolate, broken
- 75g flour
- 1 tsp baking powder
- 3 tbsp cocoa
- 250g whole almonds, skin on, or 250g ground almonds
- 8 eggs, separated
- 300g golden caster sugar
- Clementine slices and whipped cream or vanilla ice cream, to serve

Honey-roasted almonds
- 200g flaked almonds
- 3 tbsp honey

Chocolate ganache icing
- 200g double cream
- 200g 70%-cocoa chocolate, broken

1 Unwrap the butter and use the paper to grease the insides of two 24cm springform cake tins. Line the base of each tin with a circle of greaseproof paper. Preheat the oven to 180C/gas 4.
2 Melt the chocolate and butter in a heatproof bowl over a pan of barely

EPIC BROWNIE GATEAU

CHOCOLATE TART WITH SALT FLAKES

CHOCOLATE TART WITH SALT FLAKES

Serves 4-6

- 300ml double cream
- 2 tsp caster sugar
- A pinch of fine sea salt
- 50g unsalted butter, softened
- 200g 70% cocoa chocolate, broken into small pieces
- 50ml whole milk
- 375g shortcrust pastry
- Sea salt flakes and cream or crème fraîche, to serve

1 Preheat the oven to 180/gas 4. Roll out the pastry and line a 23cm greased tart tin. Bake blind for 10–15 minutes, then remove beans and bake again for 15 minutes until golden.
2 Put the cream, sugar and salt in a pan and bring to the boil. Remove as soon as the mixture boils. Off the heat, add the butter and chocolate. Stir until blended.
3 Allow the chocolate 10 minutes to cool, then stir in the milk. Keep stirring until your mixture is nice and shiny. Pour into the tart shell and leave at room temperature for 2 hours to set.
4 Sprinkle the salt flakes all over, then serve with crème fraîche.

GRILLED PINEAPPLE WITH SPICED SALT

Serves 4

- Vegetable oil or rapeseed oil
- 1 ripe pineapple, peeled and cut into slices
- 2 tbsp caster sugar
- A pinch of spiced or chilli salt

1 Rub a griddle pan with oil and heat to medium-hot. Sprinkle the pineapple slices with the caster sugar and cook, sugar-side down, for 8 minutes. Turn, sprinkle lightly with the spiced salt and cook for another few minutes.

GRILLED PINEAPPLE WITH SPICED SALT

RHUBARB TARTLET

Not pictured

Serves 6

- 750g rhubarb, cut into 6cm pieces
- 300g sugar
- Zest and juice of 1 orange
- 1 vanilla pod, split, seeds scraped
- 375g puff pastry
- 1 egg, beaten with a dash of milk

1 Preheat the oven to 200C/gas 6. Poach the rhubarb in 200ml water with the sugar, orange zest and juice and vanilla pod and seeds. After 5 minutes, lift out of the syrup and leave to cool, reserving the syrup.
2 Roll out the pastry to just larger than an A4 sheet of paper. Score the pastry, leaving a 2cm border. Brush the edges of the pastry with the egg wash. Lay the rhubarb in the scored pastry and bake for 20–25 minutes, until golden. Reduce the syrup in the pan, then drizzle over tart when cooked.

RICOTTA CAKE

Not pictured

Serves 8

- 175g butter, plus extra
- 200g self-raising flour, plus extra
- 175g caster sugar
- Zest of 2 oranges
- 3 eggs, separated
- 250g best-quality ricotta
- 1 tsp baking powder
- 8 tbsp orange-flower water
- 2 handfuls of crushed shortbread

1 Heat the oven to 180C/gas 4. Butter a 21cm spring-form cake tin. Beat the butter and sugar till light, then beat in the zest, yolks and ricotta. Whisk the egg whites till stiff, then fold into the ricotta mix. Fold in the flour, baking powder and half the orange flower; then spoon the mixture into the tin. Bake for 35 minutes, till risen and golden. Cool for 30 minutes in the tin. Top with the remaining orange flower and the crushed shortbread.

PEAR & CHOCOLATE TART

PEAR & CHOCOLATE TART
Serves 10
- 185g dark chocolate
- 125g unsalted butter
- 125g ground almonds
- 95g caster sugar
- 2 eggs, beaten
- 4 poached pears, halved
- Crème fraîche, to serve

Pastry
- 115g caster sugar
- 345g butter
- 6 egg yolks
- 575g plain flour

1 For the pastry, beat the butter and the sugar. Add the yolks and stir to combine. Add the flour and combine until you get a ball of dough. Wrap in clingfilm and chill for 30 minutes.
2 Preheat the oven to 160C/gas 2-3. Grease a loose-bottomed 28cm tart tin. Dust a clean surface with flour and roll out the chilled dough so that it's big enough to line the tin. Lightly press the pastry into the tin and trim any excess. Line the pastry with greaseproof paper, then fill it with rice or dried beans. Bake for 15 minutes. Remove the paper and beans and return to the oven for another 15 minutes or until golden. Remove from the oven and cool.
3 Gently melt the chocolate. Cream the butter, almonds, eggs and sugar and fold in the melted chocolate. Spoon the mixture into the tart case and push the pears down into it. Bake for 40 minutes. Serve cool with crème fraîche.

LEMON RIPPLE TART
Serves 10
- 6 egg yolks
- 5 eggs
- 270g caster sugar
- 1 vanilla pod, split lengthways, seeds removed
- 250ml lemon juice, plus the grated zest from the lemons
- 250g butter, at room temperature
- 250g raspberries
- 1 tbsp caster sugar
- Icing sugar for caramelising (optional)

Pastry
- 500g plain flour, plus extra
- 100g icing sugar
- 250g unsalted cold butter, cubed
- Finely grated zest of 1 lemon
- 2 eggs, beaten with a splash of milk

1 For the pastry, sieve the flour and icing sugar onto a surface, then use your fingers to gently work in the butter till you have 'crumbs'. Sprinkle in the zest, then gradually add the egg mixture till you get a ball of dough. Dust with flour, flatten slightly, then wrap in clingfilm and chill for about 30 minutes.
2 Grease a loose-bottomed 28cm tart tin. Dust a clean surface and roll the pastry into a circle that's 5mm thick and big enough to line the tin. Lightly press the pastry into the tin, trim off any excess, then cover with clingfilm and put in the freezer for an hour.
3 Preheat the oven to 180C/gas 4. Unwrap the tart case, line it with greaseproof paper, then fill with rice or dried beans. Bake the pastry in the middle of the oven for 10 minutes, then remove the paper and beans and return to the oven for 15 minutes till golden.
4 For the filling, put the yolks, eggs, sugar, vanilla seeds and lemon juice and zest into a heavy-bottomed pan; whisk over a very low heat until the mixture starts to thicken. Stir in the butter, making sure you get all the bits of curd from the bottom of the pan. When it looks like really thick custard and coats the back of a spoon, take it off the heat and let it cool a little. Give it a whisk, then strain through a sieve.
5 Mash the raspberries with the sugar in a small pan. Cook over medium heat for 10 minutes, until it looks like jam.
6 Spoon the lukewarm lemon into the tart and shake it so that the mixture spreads evenly. Spoon the raspberry over the lemon and gently stir it to create a ripple effect. Cool the tart for 30 minutes. If you want, sprinkle with icing sugar and carefully caramelise the surface with a kitchen blowtorch.

TRADITIONAL CHRISTMAS CAKE

TRADITIONAL CHRISTMAS CAKE

This is best made at least two months in advance.

Serves 16

- 600g raisins
- 200g currants
- 100g dried sour or glacé cherries
- 250g mixed dried fruits (try prunes, apricots, apples, pears), all finely chopped
- 400ml booze, plus extra to 'feed' the cake (brandy, sherry, Tia Maria or rum)
- 300g butter, at room temperature
- 200g dark brown sugar
- 1 lemon
- 4 eggs, at room temperature
- 2 tbsp treacle
- 300g plain flour
- ½ tsp ground ginger
- 1 tsp ground cinnamon
- A pinch of ground cloves
- 150g ground almonds
- 150g walnuts, chopped

1 The night before, place the dried fruit in a saucepan with the booze and bring to a simmer. Pour into a bowl, cool, cover and leave to soften.
2 The following day, preheat the oven to 150C/gas 2 and line the base and sides of a 23cm round tin with a double layer of greaseproof paper. Make the side lining 8cm higher than the tin.
3 Blitz half the soaked fruit in a food processor to make a paste, and stir back into the rest of the fruit. Cream the butter and sugar until light. Grate in the lemon zest and beat in the eggs, one at a time. Mix in the treacle. Sift the flour and combine with the spices and ground almonds. Mix into the butter mixture, alternating with the soaked fruit. Finally, fold in the walnuts. Spoon the mixture into the lined tin and bake in the oven for 3 hours. Check after 2½ hours, then every 20 minutes, or until a skewer comes out clean.
4 As soon as the cake comes out of the oven, brush with a little more booze. Leave to cool in the tin for 5 minutes and then remove, placing it directly onto a large sheet of tin foil. Wrap it up twice to retain the heat for as long as possible. After a few hours, remove the foil and wrap up the cake again in a double sheet of greaseproof paper and a double sheet of foil, making sure you can access the cake from the top. Store for between 2 and 12 weeks in an airtight container. During this time, feed the cake the alcohol of your choice by gently pouring it over the top and rewrapping.

CHAI MUFFINS

These vegan cupcakes are easy to make and the perfect sweet accompaniment to a steaming cup of fragrant chai.

Makes 12

- 75ml groundnut oil
- 100g caster sugar
- 175g plain flour
- 2 tsp baking powder
- ½ tsp cinnamon
- A pinch of grated nutmeg
- ½ tsp ground cardamom seeds
- 300g apple sauce
- Cinammon sticks, crumbled, to decorate (optional)

Spicy icing
- 4 chai tea bags
- 200g sugar
- 250g dairy-free sunflower spread (available in supermarkets)

1 Preheat the oven to 190/gas 5. In a bowl, thoroughly combine the oil and sugar. Add all the remaining dry ingredients, plus a pinch of salt, and mix well. Stir in the apple sauce. Spoon the batter into 12 muffin cases and bake for 15–20 minutes until golden. Transfer muffins to a wire rack to cool.
2 For the icing, put the tea bags in 200ml boiling water. After 15 minutes, remove the bags and stir in the sugar. Bring to the boil, without stirring, then simmer for 5–8 minutes. Leave to cool, then beat into the sunflower spread. Refrigerate the icing to firm up, then spread over the cooled muffins. Decorate with crumbled cinnamon sticks, if desired.

VEGAN

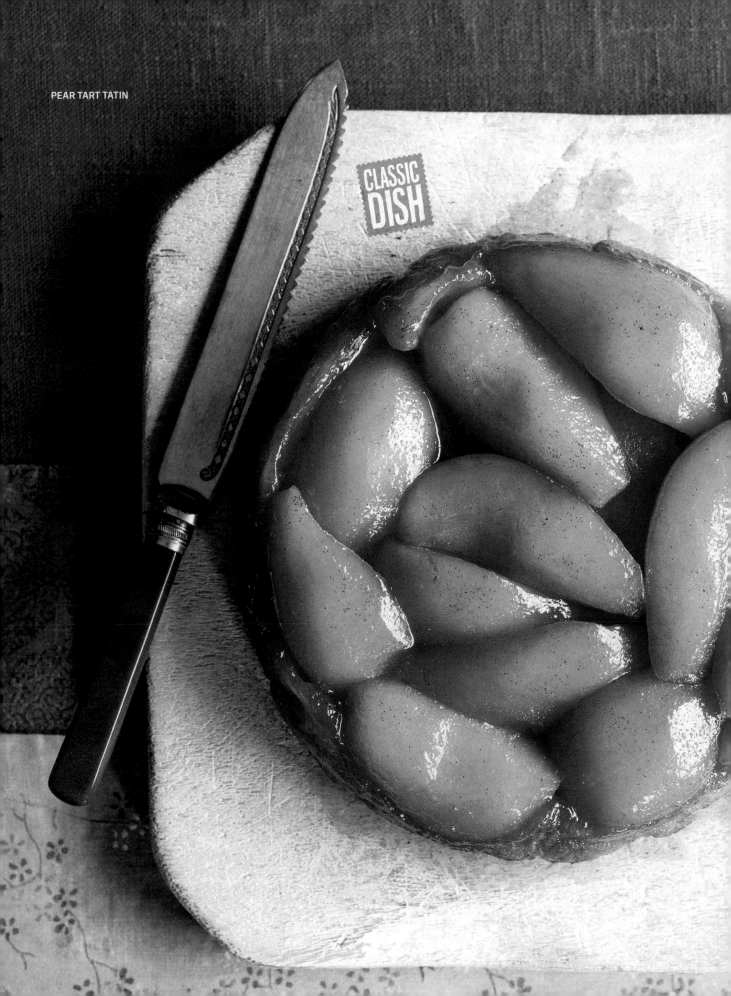

CLASSIC DISH

STUFFED FRUIT CRUMBLE

GINGER & LEMON PUDDINGS

PEAR TART TATIN

Serves 6-8

- 125g caster sugar
- 40g unsalted cold butter, chopped
- ½ tsp ground ginger
- ½ tsp ground cinnamon
- 3 large pears, peeled, cored and cut into wedges
- 375g all-butter puff pastry
- Double cream, to serve

1 Preheat the oven to 200C/gas 6. Place a 21cm ovenproof frying pan over a medium heat. Add the sugar and heat to a caramel colour, stirring constantly. Stir in the butter, ginger and cinnamon.
2 Place the pears in the caramel and spoon over the mixture. Turn down the heat and cook for 5-10 minutes, until the pears are tender but retain their shape. Remove from the heat and cool. Arrange the pears prettily in the pan.
3 Roll out the puff pastry to about 5mm thick and cut a disc slightly bigger than your pan. Place the pastry disc on top of the pears, then carefully tuck it snugly around the outside of the pears. Bake the for 30-40 minutes, or until the pastry is golden brown and puffed up.
4 Remove from the oven and leave for 10 minutes. Run a knife around the edge, place a large plate over the top and carefully turn the tart onto the plate. Serve with double cream.

STUFFED FRUIT CRUMBLE

Serves 4

- 3 cardamom pods, seeds only
- 75g caster sugar
- 70g desiccated coconut
- ½ vanilla pod, split, seeds scraped
- 1 egg white
- Zest of 1 orange, juice of half
- 4 large plums (or any soft stone fruit), halved and stoned
- Vanilla ice cream, to serve

1 Preheat the oven to 180C/gas 4. Grind the cardamom seeds in a mortar to a powder. Pour into a bowl and mix with the sugar, coconut, vanilla seeds, egg white, orange zest and juice.
2 Place the plums cut-side up on a baking tray. Pile the coconut mixture into the holes. Bake for 15-18 minutes, till the crumble is golden brown and the fruit soft. Serve with vanilla ice cream.

....

GINGER & LEMON PUDDINGS

Serves 8

- 2 eggs, separated
- 100g caster sugar
- Zest of 2 lemons
- 250ml cold milk
- 175g self-raising flour, sifted
- ¼ tsp ground cinnamon
- ½ tsp ground ginger
- 4 pieces of stem ginger
- 50g unsalted butter, melted

Syrup & topping

- 4 tbsp stem-ginger syrup
- 1 orange
- 1 lemon
- 1 piece stem ginger, finely chopped
- 2 tbsp caster sugar

1 Preheat the oven to 190C/gas 5. Beat the egg yolks, sugar and zest until pale. Beat in the milk gradually, then fold in the flour, cinnamon, ground and stem ginger and the butter. Beat till smooth. Whisk the egg whites into stiff peaks, then fold into the mixture. Spoon into 8 ramekins or ovenproof teacups. Place in a roasting tin and fill halfway up the sides with hot water. Bake for 40 minutes, or till risen and a skewer comes out clean.
2 Meanwhile, make the syrup. Place the ginger syrup in a pan with thick strips of zest cut from half the orange and half the lemon.Bring to the boil, then leave to cool and infuse. Thickly grate the rest of the zest, place in a bowl with the ginger and toss through the sugar to crystallise.
4 Brush the puddings with the cooled syrup and top with crystallised ginger and zest. Serve with custard (citrus custard is even better: add a little citrus zest when making custard, then whisk in a little juice when it's off the heat).

Peachy keen

If you're not crazy about plums, you can make the tartlets (left) and the sorbet (right) with peaches, nectarines or apricots. Stone fruit is great to cook with. Peel and quarter peaches, place in a big bowl, just cover in sweet fizzy wine such as moscato, add sugar to taste, and have as a refreshing dessert. Slice nectarines and grill till char marks appear, then drizzle with honey, sprinkle with flaked almonds and serve with yoghurt. Place apricot halves on the bottom of a cake tin, sprinkle them with sugar and spread with sponge cake mixture, then bake. For a clafoutis, pour a simple, thin batter over peach slices in a dish then bake until set. Even easier, pour good-quality ready-made custard over sweet stone-fruit slices, sprinkle with demerara sugar, then place under a hot grill to caramelise the sugar.

PLUM SORBET

PLUM TARTLETS

These little tarts will impress everybody. The sharp sweetness of the plums is perfectly offset by the rich creaminess of the ricotta. The vin santo gives them a good boozy kick.

Makes 4

- 20g butter, plus extra for greasing
- Flour, for dusting
- 250g shortcrust pastry
- 8 plums, stoned and quartered
- 100ml vin santo or dessert wine
- 50g icing sugar
- 2 eggs, separated
- Zest of ½ lemon
- 1 tbsp vanilla sugar
- 100g ricotta
- 4 tbsp plum jam

1 Grease 4 loose-bottomed, 12cm tart tins with butter. Dust your work surface with flour and roll out the pastry to about 3mm thick. Line each tin with pastry and prick the base of each with a fork a couple of times, then refrigerate for 30 minutes. Preheat the oven to 180C/gas 4. Bake the pastry cases for 15–20 minutes, until cooked and golden brown. Take out the oven and allow to cool.
2 Place the plums in a bowl and cover with the vin santo. Cream the butter and the icing sugar and gently beat in the egg yolks, lemon zest, vanilla sugar and ricotta. Whisk the egg whites until stiff, then fold into the ricotta mixture.
3 Spread a tablespoon of filling over the base of each tart tin and press in 4 plum quarters. Spread over another layer of filling, followed by another layer of fruit. Melt the jam with 2 tablespoons of water and use to brush the top plum pieces. Bake for 5 minutes, then brush the tarts again with the jam glaze and bake for another 8–12 minutes, or until the filling has turned golden. Serve the tartlets slightly warm with cream, or even better, plum sorbet.

PLUM SORBET

Makes about 750g

- 8–10 plums, stoned and quartered
- 200g sugar
- 1 egg white
- Juice of ½ lemon

1 Combine the plums and half the sugar in a large heatproof bowl. Cover tightly with clingfilm and set over a pan of simmering water to release the plum juices – about 30 minutes. Sieve the plums, gently pressing down, to give about 300ml juice – top with a little water if need be.
2 Make a sugar syrup by dissolving the remaining sugar in 100ml boiling water. Pour the syrup into the plum juice and stir to combine.
3 Beat the egg white until frothy, then squeeze in the lemon juice and stir into the plum juice. Taste, add more syrup if necessary. Churn in an ice-cream maker according to the instructions.

ROSE-WATER MADELEINES

Flavour 3 – White chocolate & green tea

- 70g white chocolate
- A knob of butter
- 1½ tsp matcha green tea powder
- 200ml double cream
- 25g caster sugar

1 Preheat the oven to 200C/gas 6. Place the butter in a saucepan, along with 250ml water and a pinch of sea salt. Heat gently, stirring until melted.
2 Bring the butter to the boil, then quickly beat in the flour until you have a smooth paste. Beat in the eggs .
3 Line a couple of baking trays with greaseproof paper and spoon your choux pastry into a piping bag. (If you don't have one, put the dough into a sandwich bag, then cut off a corner). Squeeze the mixture into 7cm-long pieces, leaving a decent gap between each one, as they'll double in size.
4 Place in the oven and bake for around 30 minutes or until golden and hard. Transfer to a wire rack and slice down the sides of each eclair so the steam can escape. Cool while you make the fillings.
5 For the strawberry filling, melt the chocolate and butter in a bowl over a pan of simmering water, stir, then cool slightly. Toss the strawberries through the sugar, mashing a little. Add the vanilla seeds to the cream and whisk into soft peaks, then stir in the strawberry mix. Fill the eclairs with the cream mixture and spoon the melted chocolate over the top.
6 For the chocolate-cardamom filling, melt the chocolate in a bowl over a pan of simmering water with the knob of butter, stir, then cool. Bash the cardamom seeds, discard the shells, and grind the black seeds until fine. Add to the cream with the sugar and whisk into soft peaks. Fill the eclairs with the cream mixture and spoon the melted chocolate over the top.
7 For the green tea filling, melt the white chocolate in a bowl over a pan of simmering water with the butter, stir, then cool. Mix the tea powder into 1 tbsp of hot water to form a paste. Whisk the cream to soft peaks with the sugar, then stir through the paste. Fill the buns with the cream and spoon over the melted chocolate.

ROSE-WATER MADELEINES

You'll need special madeleine moulds to make these distinctive pastries.

Makes 18
- 125g butter
- 2 eggs
- 100g caster sugar
- 100g plain flour, sieved
- Juice and zest of ½ lemon
- 2 tbsp rose water
- 100g icing sugar
- Dried rose petals (optional)

1 Preheat the oven to 190C/gas 5. Melt the butter in a pan. Use a little to grease your moulds and leave the rest to cool.
2 Beat the eggs and sugar till fluffy. Fold in the flour using a metal spoon. Stir in the butter, zest and half the rose water. Spoon into your moulds and bake for 8 minutes, or till golden.
3 Sift the icing sugar into a bowl and stir in the remaining rose water and enough lemon juice to thin. Turn the cakes out onto a wire rack to cool, then drizzle with icing and sprinkle with dried rose petals.

ECLAIRS THREE WAYS

Makes 22-24 eclairs
- 100g butter, cut into cubes
- 140g plain flour
- 3 eggs, beaten

Flavour 1 – Strawberries & cream
- 70g dark chocolate
- A knob of butter
- A handful of strawberries, hulled and chopped
- 50g caster sugar
- 1 vanilla pod, seeds scraped
- 200ml double cream

Flavour 2 – Chocolate & cardamom
- 70g milk chocolate
- A knob of butter
- 1 tsp cardamom pods
- 200ml double cream
- 25g caster sugar

ECLAIRS THREE WAYS

CHOCOLATE, CRANBERRY & ORANGE BISCUITS

PISTACHIO & SAFFRON BISCOTTI

If you like, substitute almonds for pistachios and vanilla for saffron.

Makes about 50

- 180g pistachios
- A good pinch of saffron threads
- 110g unsalted butter
- 3 eggs
- 200g caster sugar
- 630g plain flour
- 1 tsp baking powder

1 Preheat the oven to 180C/gas 4. Spread the pistachios on a baking tray and bake for 5 minutes. Once slightly coloured, remove and leave to cool.
2 Soak the saffron in 2 tablespoons of boiling water. In an electric mixer, beat the butter until light and fluffy. With the mixer running, gradually add the eggs, sugar, saffron threads and soaking water, and mix until creamed. Gently add in the flour and baking powder, along with a good pinch of salt. Mix the dough until smooth and stir in the pistachios.
3 Line and grease a large tray or 2 smaller ones and shape your dough into long logs about 2cm high – not too high, but you can make it wide for larger biscotti or thin for smaller ones. Bake for 30 minutes or until golden. Let the logs cool for 5 minutes then place on a cutting board. Diagonally slice each log into 2cm-thick pieces. Place back on the tray, cut-sides up, and bake for 5 minutes, or till golden. Turn them over and bake for another 5 minutes. When cooked, allow to cool on a rack, then store in an airtight container.

CHOCOLATE, CRANBERRY & ORANGE BISCUITS

Makes about 20

- 75g butter
- 100g golden caster sugar
- 1 egg
- Zest of ½ orange
- 160g plain flour
- ½ tsp baking powder
- A pinch of salt
- 50g dried cranberries
- 100g dark chocolate, chopped

1 Preheat the oven to 190C/gas 5. Cream the butter and sugar, then mix in the egg and the orange zest. Stir in the flour, baking powder and a pinch of salt. Stir in the cranberries and chocolate pieces. Place pound coin-sized dollops of the mixture, well spaced, on baking trays lined with parchment paper. Bake for 12-15 minutes or until golden. Eat with hot chocolate or a mug of tea.

GREAT AS A GIFT

PISTACHIO & SAFFRON BISCOTTI

Years in the making

Serve Zacapa rum at the end of a meal and you're not just serving any old digestif. Zacapa hails from Guatemala in central America. Here, the tropical lowland soils yield an ultra-high-grade sugar cane, from which Zacapa uses just the first pressing, or 'virgin sugar cane honey'.

Zacapa 23 is a blend of rums aged for between 6 and 23 years in oak, using casks that previously held robust bourbons and delicate sherries, each of which imparts its own distinct flavour signature. Under the expert eye of master blender Lorena Vasquez, the rum is matured in a Sistema Solera system, as used for sherry, which guarantees the quality of the finished spirit.

Zacapa XO follows this same premium production process, before spending a further two years in fine French cognac barrels – which explains its nickname, 'the Cognac of Rums'.

The result of all this time, care and expertise are two wonderfully complex and beautifully balanced drinks. Zacapa 23 is a swirl of honey, butterscotch, spiced oak and dried fruit flavours with a deep, long aftertaste, while XO reveals wisps of vanilla, almonds and burnt caramel on the nose and notes of dark cherry chocolate, dried fruits and sweet oak in the mouth.

As you'd expect from such noble spirits, you don't want to mask their flavours with mixers. Both are best served simply, with nothing more than the odd ice cube to tease out their aromas.

Drinks

It's time to get glugging. Head for the sunshine with a watermelon glory (page 149) or a Carribean frappé (page 152). Refresh yourself with an alcohol-free tutti-frutti cordial (page 151) or a planter's punchless and settle in on a winter's evening with a mulled cider (page 153) or a spiced hot chocolate (page 150)

WATERMELON GLORY

HONEY PINA COLADA

WATERMELON GLORY

Serves 2

- 2 shots golden rum, such as Pampero Especial
- 400g watermelon flesh
- 1–2 tbsp vanilla syrup, to taste
- Slices of watermelon, to serve

1 Blitz the rum, watermelon and syrup with some ice cubes in a blender. Pour into glasses and serve immediatly with watermelon slices to garnish.

MULLED VODKA

This makes a lovely gift.

Makes 1 litre

- 1 litre vodka
- 50g blanched almonds
- 40g soft dark brown sugar
- 2 tbsp honey
- 2 cinnamon sticks
- 6 cloves
- 1 star anise
- 2 bay leaves
- 1 vanilla pod, seeds scraped
- Peel from 1 orange and 1 lemon, in thick strips, pith removed

1 Sterilise a 1.25 litre bottle. Place all the ingredients inside and give it a good shake. Seal and store for at least 2 weeks, shaking it every week.

2 Present the vodka in the bottle, with all the ingredients showing. It is delicious served on the rocks, or in a long glass with warm apple juice.

HONEY PINA COLADA

Serves 4

- 2 tsp honey, plus extra to serve
- Flesh of ½ pineapple, plus extra to serve
- 200ml pineapple juice
- 4 shots each golden rum (such as Pampero Especial), coconut milk and single cream

1 Blend the honey, pineapple and juice with ice in a blender until smooth. Stir in the other ingredients. Serve in glasses with an extra pineapple slice and a little honey drizzled over the top.

APRICOT CORDIAL

Makes 500ml

- 500g ripe apricots, stoned and roughly chopped
- 300g golden caster sugar
- 2 lemons, juiced
- Soda water or prosecco, to fill

1 Place the apricots in a pan with the sugar, lemon juice and 300ml water. Bring to the boil, then simmer for 15 minutes, till it forms a syrup and the fruit breaks down. Leave to cool, then sieve. Bottle the syrup and keep in the fridge or pour 2 tablespoons into a glass and top with soda water or prosecco.

JAMIE'S ITALIAN'S ESPRESSO MARTINI

Sweet and strong, this is the perfect after-dinner drink.

Serves 1

- ½ shot chilled espresso
- ¼ shot sugar syrup
- ½ shot Kahlua
- 1 shot vodka

1 Combine all the ingredients in a cocktail shaker with plenty of ice cubes. Shake vigorously until there is a frothy head. Strain and pour into a chilled martini glass and garnish by floating a couple of coffee beans on the top.

CIDER CUP

Serves 2

- ½ lemon, sliced
- ½ orange, sliced
- 1 apple, sliced
- 500ml dry cider, chilled

1 Divide the fruit between 2 tall glasses and top with cider and ice cubes.

FIG & GIN COCKTAIL

In a muddle

All mixed up over this term? Muddling is an easy bar technique for combining cocktail ingredients before adding liquid. Add fruit and sugar to a cocktail shaker or tall, wide glass and pound with a muddler or a wooden spoon until well combined, then add the alcohol. Use this technique with limes, mint and sugar before adding cachaça to make a caipirinha. Pound up blackberries with sugar and lemon, pour over ice and top up with Tanqueray gin. Bash pineapple, ginger and lemongrass with chilli (if you dare!) and top up with vodka and ginger beer. Mango is lovely muddled with passionfruit before adding Pampero rum, sugar syrup and mint. Crush peaches and raspberries and top up with prosecco; mash stawberries, then add a dash of crème de cassis and a pour of fizz.

FIG & GIN COCKTAIL
Serves 4
- 6 figs
- 200ml gin, such as Tanqueray
- 4 tbsp gooseberry jam
- 300ml bitter lemon

1 Remove the stalks from 5 of the figs and blitz in a blender with the gin and jam. Pour into 4 glasses, top with the bitter lemon, give it a good stir and add a few ice cubes. Slice the remaining fig into thin wedges and use to garnish.

SPICED HOT CHOCOLATE
Serves 1
- 250-300ml milk
- 4-5 cloves
- 1 cinnamon stick
- Nutmeg, for grating
- 2 tbsp cocoa
- 2-3 tbsp caster or vanilla sugar

1 In a pan, heat the milk with the cloves, cinnamon and a grating of nutmeg for 5 minutes. In another pan, mix the cocoa with 1 tablespoon of hot milk into a paste. Whisk in the rest of the milk. Add the sugar and heat till almost boiling, then strain into a mug.

POMOJITO
Serves 1
- 4 mint leaves, plus 1 sprig to decorate
- 15ml lime juice
- 25ml sugar syrup (50:50 sugar and water simmered for 5 minutes)
- Crushed ice
- 45ml white rum, such as Pampero Blanco
- 30ml pomegranate juice, such as Pom Wonderful
- Soda water, to fill

1 In an old-fashioned glass, bruise the mint with the lime juice and sugar syrup. Add the crushed ice, followed by the rum and pomegranate juice. Top with a splash of soda and stir, then decorate with the mint sprig to serve.

FROZEN MANGO DAIQUIRI
With its use of white rum and tropical fruit, this fruity cocktail is full of the flavours of Jamaica.
Serves 1
- Flesh of 1 ripe mango, chopped
- 1 shot white rum, such as Pampero Blanco
- 1 tsp sugar syrup (50:50 sugar and water, simmered for 5 minutes)

1 Whizz the ingredients together with a few ice cubes in a blender till smooth. Taste to check the sweetness, adding more sugar syrup if needed. Pour into a tall glass and top with ice. You can omit the rum for a non-alcoholic smoothie.

ST CLEMENTS, A TUTTI-FRUTTI CORDIAL

GINGER & MINT LIMEADE

ST CLEMENTS, A TUTTI-FRUTTI CORDIAL

This sweet and zippy citrus-fruit syrup can be topped up with soda water for the young or virtuous, or with a more fun fizz for the rest of us.

Makes about 1.5 litres

- 6 oranges, zested with a peeler
- 6 lemons, zested with a peeler
- 6 mandarins, zested with a peeler
- 400g golden caster sugar
- 2 vanilla pods, seeds scraped
- 4 bay leaves
- Fizzy water, prosecco or cava, to serve

1 Juice all the fruit and pour into a big pan, along with the strips of fruit zest, the sugar, the vanilla seeds and pods, bay leaves and 300ml water. Bring to the boil, then remove from heat, cover and leave to steep for 30 minutes or longer if you wish.
2 Pour the cordial into sterilised bottles, poking in the bay leaves, vanilla pods and some of the zest, if you like – this gives the cordial a little bit of extra flavour and makes it look pretty. Keep refrigerated until required; it can be kept for up to 2 weeks.
3 To serve, fill glasses about one-third full with cordial and top up with fizzy water or sparkling wine.

GINGER & MINT LIMEADE

Makes 250ml of syrup

- 125g sugar
- 125ml water
- A small handful of mint leaves
- A large piece of ginger, sliced
- Soda water, lime juice and wedges and mint leaves, to serve

1 Place the sugar and water in a pan, together with the mint and the ginger slices. Place on a hob over a high heat and bring to the boil. Lower the heat and simmer for 10 minutes, until reduced but not coloured. Allow to cool, then refrigerate. This will keep in the fridge for up to a week.
2 To serve, mix the chilled syrup to taste with some lime juice and top with soda water. Gently stir to combine, add some ice cubes and garnish with mint and a lime wedge. Add a couple of shots of rum, gin or vodka if you're in the mood.

CUCUMBER, RASPBERRY & GIN COCKTAIL

Serves 2

- A large handful of raspberries
- 5cm piece of cucumber, chopped
- A few mint leaves
- 100ml gin, such as Tanqueray
- 1 tbsp sugar
- Bitter lemon, to fill

1 In a cocktail shaker, bash the berries, cucumber and mint with a wooden muddler or a spoon. Add the gin and sugar. Bash a little more, then add some ice. Shake well, then strain between 2 glasses. Top with bitter lemon.

BLOODY MARY MIX

Serve this mix as it is, as a virgin mary, or with alcohol as a bloody mary. If you're using the sherry, make sure it's dry. A fino such as Tio Pepe is ideal.

Serves 4

- 1 litre tomato juice
- 1cm-piece of fresh horseradish, peeled and grated
- Juice of ½ lemon
- ½ tsp Tabasco sauce
- 1 tsp worcestershire sauce
- Celery salt and celery sticks, and lemon wedges, to serve
- Chilled vodka and dry sherry (optional)

1 Combine all the ingredients in a jug, season to taste and chill in the fridge.
2 When you're ready to serve, pour the mix into chilled glasses, adding a little ice, a sprinkle of celery salt and a celery stick, and 1–2 shots of vodka and a splash of sherry, if desired.

CARIBBEAN FRAPPE

VIRGIN APPLE MOJITO

CARIBBEAN FRAPPE

Irish Moss is a popular drink in Jamaica and is available in some shops in the UK, though if you can't find it you can use diluted condensed milk instead.
Serves 4

- Crushed ice, to serve
- 4 shots white rum, such as Pampero Blanco
- 4 shots espresso coffee
- 1 x 284ml can Irish moss

1 Fill 4 highball glasses with crushed ice. Add a shot of white rum and a shot of espresso to each glass; top up with Irish Moss. Stir before drinking.

VIRGIN APPLE MOJITO

Serves 1

- 12 mint leaves
- 15ml lime juice
- 50ml freshly pressed apple juice
- 20ml sugar syrup (50:50 sugar and water, simmered for 5 minutes)
- Crushed ice, to serve
- Ginger ale, to fill

1 Muddle the mint in your glass. Add the lime and apple juices and sugar syrup. Half fill the glass with crushed ice and muddle some more. Stir and top up with ginger ale.

SUMMER GIN CUP

Recipe by Nick Strangeway
Cups and punches were popular during the late 18th and early 19th centuries. This recipe is inspired by a cup invented in the mid-19th century by James Pimm at his restaurant in London. He later bottled his concoction of gin blended with liqueurs, herbs and spices. It remains the definitive English summer drink.
Makes as much as you like!

- A mix of fruit - try using lemon and orange slices, diced strawberries, whole raspberries, and cucumber cut into wheels
- 4 parts gin
- 3 parts lemon juice
- 1 part crème de cassis
- 1 part sweet vermouth, such as Martini Rosso or Noilly Prat Rouge
- ½ part elderflower cordial
- A dash of Angostura bitters
- Soda water, homemade lemonade or prosecco, to fill
- Mint and ice, to serve

1 Add all the ingredients, except the fizzy element, to a punch bowl or pitcher and stir well. If you've got time, allow the fruit to steep in the alcohol for a few hours. Add ice and top with the fizz of your choice. Garnish with mint and ladle into ice-filled glasses.

ORCHARD MOJITO

Recipe by Nick Strangeway
While Prohibition held sway in the USA, Cuba was where it was at and the Floridita was the island's pre-eminent bar. In the Floridita's cocktail book, the Mojito No #2 is made not with rum, but with gin. For a summery version, use elderflower cordial rather than sugar syrup, while in autumn, top with ginger beer instead of soda.
Serves 1

- 8–10 mint leaves
- 15ml sugar syrup (50:50 sugar and water, simmered for 5 minutes)
- 25ml lime juice
- 50ml gin
- 50ml pressed apple juice
- Soda water, to fill
- A slice of apple, to serve

1 To build the drink in a highball glass, bruise the mint in the sugar syrup and then add the lime, gin and apple juice. Add cubed ice to fill the glass. Give it all a stir and top with the soda water and garnish with mint and a slice of apple.

INCREDIBLE MULLED CIDER

It's not hard to make this from scratch. Just pick up a few bottles of decent scrumpy and give it a try.

Serves 15

- 2 litres good-quality traditional cider
- 6 cloves
- 3-4 star anise
- ¼ nutmeg finely grated into the pan
- 1 cinnamon stick
- 1 vanilla pod, halved
- Juice of 1 orange
- Juice of 2 clementines
- Juice and seeds of 1 pomegranate
- 4-5 tbsp caster sugar

1 Pour the cider into a large saucepan on a low heat and let it warm through for a few minutes. Add all the spices and juices and turn up the heat. Once it is boiling, turn down to a simmer and leave to tick away for 5-8 minutes. As everything infuses you'll get delicious layers of flavour. Taste it and add as much sugar as you like. When you're happy with the flavours, ladle into glasses or mugs and serve while warm.

INCREDIBLE MULLED CIDER

OREO MILKSHAKE

Serves 1

- 200ml ice-cold milk
- 1 scoop of vanilla ice cream
- 3 Oreo cookies

1 Throw everything into a blender and blitz. Serve immediately. You can add a little extra ice cream if you're feeling daring, or add a few shots of Baileys if you're feeling dangerous.

BLACKBERRY BLOODHOUND

Recipe by Nick Strangeway

There was a time about 15 years ago when any drink served in a cocktail glass was called a martini. Fresh fruit martinis - vodka shaken with fresh fruit - became especially fashionable. However a much superior drink, the bloodhound, reached our shores from America in the 1920s, courtesy of the Duke of Manchester, or so they say.

Serves 1

- 50ml gin
- 15ml Noilly Rouge
- 10ml Noilly Prat
- 5ml sugar syrup (50:50 sugar and water, simmered for 5 minutes)
- 8 blackberries, plus a few to serve

1 Shake all the ingredients together in a cocktail shaker and finely strain into a chilled cocktail glass to serve. Garnish with a couple of blackberries.

COSMOPOLITAN DAISY

Recipe by Nick Strangeway

We're familiar with the vodka cosmopolitan, but before Prohibition, a similar drink was made using gin.

Serves 1

- 6 raspberries
- 50ml gin
- 20ml Cointreau
- 25ml lemon juice

Raspberry syrup

- 150g raspberries
- 125ml water
- 125g caster sugar

1 For the syrup, heat the raspberries in the water. When it boils, add the sugar and stir to dissolve. Pass through a sieve, but don't push it through.
2 Crush the 6 raspberries in the syrup. Add all the ingredients to a cocktail shaker and shake everything over ice. Double strain through a fine sieve into a chilled cocktail glass.

LEMONADE SIDECAR

PLATINUM BLONDE
Serves 1
- 1 shot white rum, such as Pampero Blanco
- 1 shot Cointreau
- 1 shot single cream
- A dash of grenadine

1 Combine all the ingredients in a cocktail shaker with plenty of ice. Shake and strain into a chilled cocktail glass.

....

ALGONQUIN
Serves 1
- 2 shots rye whiskey
- 1 shot dry vermouth
- 2 shots pineapple juice
- A sliver of fresh pineapple, to garnish

1 Combine all the ingredients in a cocktail shaker with plenty of ice. Shake and strain into a chilled cocktail glass.

....

FUZZY NAVEL
Serves 1
- 1 shot vodka
- 1 shot peach brandy
- 3 shots orange juice
- A slice of fresh peach, to garnish

1 Combine all the ingredients in a cocktail shaker with plenty of ice. Shake and strain into a chilled cocktail glass filled with ice. Garnish with a slice of peach.

....

RAMOS GIN FIZZ
Serves 1
- 1½ shots gin, such as Tanqueray
- 2 shots cream
- Juice of ½ lime
- 1 egg white
- 1 tsp sugar syrup (50:50 sugar and water, simmered for 5 minutes)
- 2 drops orange-flower water
- Soda water, to fill

1 Combine all the ingredients with ice in a cocktail shaker, shake hard, then strain into a chilled cocktail glass and fill to the top with soda water.

LEMONADE SIDECAR
Makes 1
- 3 tbsp caster sugar, plus extra
- Juice of 2 lemons, plus 1-2 slices
- 150g watermelon or strawberries
- 50ml brandy
- 25ml Cointreau
- Caster sugar, to serve

1 Add 3 tablespoons of boiling water to a bowl with the sugar and stir to dissolve. Pour into a food processor (or use a hand-held blender), add the lemon juice and the fruit, then blitz. Pour into a cocktail shaker, along with the spirits. Throw in a couple of handfuls of ice, put the lid on and shake well. Have a taste, then add another squeeze of lemon juice if you like.
2 Rub a slice of lemon round the glass rim, then turn the glass upside down and press the rim in some caster sugar. Drop the lemon slices into the glass and pour in your cocktail.

MULLED WINE
This winter warmer is so delicious that it would be a shame to only drink it at Christmas. You don't want to use your best wine to make this.
Serves 6-8
- 1 bottle dry red wine
- 2-3 cinnamon sticks
- A pinch of whole cloves
- Nutmeg, for grating
- A pinch of allspice
- 1 lemon, zested, then sliced
- 1 orange, zested, then sliced
- 50g caster sugar

1 Pour the red wine into a pan and throw in the cinnamon sticks, cloves, a grating of nutmeg, the allspice, and the lemon and orange zest and slices. Add the caster sugar, then heat gently for about 10 minutes, until the sugar is dissolved. Don't let it boil or all your alcohol will evaporate. Ladle through a sieve into warm glasses to serve.

JERKY MARY

PLANTER'S PUNCHLESS

JERKY MARY

We like Walkerswood Jerk Seasoning best in this spicy Jamaican cocktail. Use as much as you see fit.
Serves 4

- 4 shots white rum, such as Pampero Blanco
- 500ml tomato juice
- 1½ tsp jerk seasoning or paste
- Juice of 1 lime
- Cucumber wedges, to serve

1 Shake the rum, 200ml tomato juice, the jerk paste and lime juice in a cocktail shaker with ice. Pour into glasses, top up with remaining tomato juice and garnish with cucumber.

FISH HOUSE PUNCH

Serves everyone at the party!

- ½ bottle dark rum
- ½ bottle brandy
- ½ bottle peach brandy
- Juice of 8 lemons
- 4 shots sugar syrup (50:50 sugar and water, simmered for 5 minutes)
- 4 peaches, skinned and chopped

1 Combine all the ingredients in a punch bowl or even your sink! Stir through ice cubes and top up with iced water until you reach your desired strength. Serve in chilled highball glasses.

SALTY DOG

Serves 1

- ½ lemon
- A handful of salt, on a saucer
- Crushed ice, to serve
- 1 shot vodka
- 2 shots grapefruit juice
- Peeled grapefruit zest, to serve

1 Rub the lemon around the edge of your glass and twist the edge in the saucer of salt. Fill the glass with the crushed ice, pour over the ingredients and garnish with the grapefruit zest.

YELLOW BIRD

Serves 1

- 1 shot golden rum, such as Pampero Especial
- 1 shot Cointreau
- 1 shot Galliano
- Juice of ½ lime
- Crushed ice

1 Whizz all the ingredients together in a blender. Pour into a chilled cocktail glass.

BRONX COCKTAIL

Serves 1

- 1 shot gin, such as Tanqueray
- 1 shot dry vermouth
- 1 shot sweet vermouth
- 2 shots orange juice
- Peeled lemon zest, to serve

1 Combine all the ingredients with lots of ice in a cocktail shaker. Shake, then strain into a chilled highball glass and garnish with a piece of lemon zest, to serve.

PLANTER'S PUNCHLESS

Serves 1

- 75ml freshly pressed apple juice
- 20ml raspberry syrup, such as Teisseire Sirop Framboise
- 15ml lime juice
- 75ml pressed white grape juice

1 Combine all the ingredients with ice in a cocktail shaker, then strain into an ice-filled tall glass.

HURRICANE

Serves 1

- 1 shot dark rum, such as Zacapa 23
- 1 shot white rum, such as Pampero Blanco
- Juice of ½ lime
- 2 shots passion fruit juice

1 Combine all the ingredients with plenty of ice in a cocktail shaker, then strain into a chilled cocktail glass.

Sauces
(and other useful stuff)

Even the most basic meal needn't be boring - it's so easy to make mustard sauce (page 160), whisky glaze (page 162), or herb pesto (page 159). Plus, extras like marinated feta (page 162), flavoured salt and sugar (pages 161 & 163) and anchovy butter (page 159) are great to have on hand to add a punch of flavour

QUICK CHERRY CHUTNEY

CANDIED PEEL

QUICK CHERRY CHUTNEY

Good with pork chops, even better with roast pork belly, as its acidity is a good foil for the fattiness of the meat.

Serves 4

- A knob of butter
- Olive oil
- 1 fennel bulb, chopped
- ½ tsp fennel seeds
- 1 onion, sliced
- 1 star anise
- 400g cherries, stoned
- 2 tbsp balsamic vinegar
- 250ml red wine

1 Add the butter and a little oil to a pan on a medium heat, then the fennel bulb and seeds, onion and star anise. Cook till the veg have softened but not coloured.
2 Add the cherries and vinegar and cook for 30 seconds, stirring. Add the wine and bring to a boil. Cook to reduce the wine, stirring, until it has a chutney-like consistency. Season to taste. Remove the star anise before serving.

CANDIED PEEL

Makes about 450g

- 2 grapefruits
- 2 oranges
- 2 lemons
- 750g granulated sugar
- About 100g caster sugar (optional)
- About 50g dark chocolate, melted (optional)

1 Stand your fruit upright and carefully cut away the peel, avoiding any pith. Slice into 5mm-wide strips, place in a saucepan with cold water, bring to the boil and simmer for about 30 minutes.
2 Meanwhile, put the granulated sugar into a pan with 400ml water and heat gently to dissolve the sugar. Bring to the boil, then remove from the heat.
3 Drain the peel and place into the hot syrup. Bring the syrup back to a simmer and cook, uncovered, for about 1 hour, until there is hardly any syrup left. Stir it to stop it sticking to the pan.
4 Line a tray with greaseproof paper. Remove the peel and place on the tray. Place in a cool place and leave to dry for a couple of days. You can then either crystallise the peel by tossing it in caster sugar, or dip it in chocolate. Store in an airtight container.

PRALINE

This is great as a sweet treat to go with your coffee or to bash up and sprinkle over ice cream.

Makes about 150g

- 180g sugar
- 100g skinned, toasted almonds

1 Put the sugar in a heavy pan on the lowest heat and leave to melt. Swirl the pan, but don't stir. Once the sugar has turned liquid and golden brown, pour in the toasted almonds, and stir well until they are all coated. When cool, break up, then store in an airtight container.

VANILLA CREAM

Makes enough for 1 medium-sized cake or 12 scones

- 300ml double cream
- 1 tbsp caster sugar
- Seeds from 1 vanilla pod or ½ tsp vanilla extract

1 Place all the ingredients in a large bowl and whisk until the cream has formed soft peaks – when it has increased in volume and just keeps its shape. Spread in the middle of your cake or serve with scones and jam.

PICKLED CHERRIES

To the sauce

A quick sauce is an easy way to pep up a simple meal. Fry garlic, onion and dried oregano, then add some tomato passata and simmer till thickened. Add chilli flakes to the garlic for a bit of a kick for pasta, or stir in a handful of olives to turn a chicken breast into instant cacciatore. A basic white sauce is made by heating 1 litre milk and 2 bay leaves in one pan while in another you melt 110g butter, then stir in 120g flour till smooth. Ladle in the milk, stirring all the while, then whisk until the sauce is thick and smooth. Now you can season with salt and pepper, and add any flavours you like – a handful or grated cheddar for a cheese sauce, or crumbled stilton for a stronger flavour. Add chopped parsley and serve with baked ham, or mustard to have with slices of beef.

PICKLED CHERRIES

Delicious with cold meats and paté, or great as a homemade gift for friends.

Makes a 700ml jar

- 450g cherries (or enough to fill your jar)
- 400ml white wine vinegar
- 150g golden caster sugar
- 2 sprigs of tarragon

1 Sterilise your jar. Trim the cherry stalks to about 1cm each. Pierce each cherry with a needle or the tip of a sharp knife in 6-8 places. Add the fruit to a saucepan with the vinegar, sugar, 1 sprig of tarragon and a pinch of salt, then bring to the boil. Simmer for 3 minutes. While hot, transfer the cherries to the jar, add the other tarragon sprig, then pour over the liquid. Seal, cool, then put in the fridge. Store for at least a fortnight before opening. Once opened, these will keep for 3 weeks, refrigerated.

FIG WHEEL

This Spanish delicacy is lovely with cheese. If you can't find fig leaves, use greaseproof paper instead.

Makes a 15cm-wheel

- 4-6 fig leaves in brine, drained (see note)
- 50g mixed blanched almonds and hazelnuts
- 250g dried figs, stems trimmed
- 1 tbsp sesame seeds
- A pinch of ground cloves
- A pinch of ground cinnamon
- 1 tbsp honey
- 2-3 tbsp sweet sherry

1 Drain the fig leaves and put in a pan of cold water, bring to the boil and simmer for 10 minutes, then drain. When cool, use the leaves to line a shallow 15cm-diameter cake tin, overlapping across the base and up the sides, leaving plenty of overhang to fold over and cover the filling afterwards. If you are using greaseproof paper instead of fig leaves, line the tin in the same way. 2 Preheat the oven to 140C/gas 1. Toast the almonds and hazelnuts in a dry pan over a medium heat for a few minutes, then roughly chop. Place the figs into a food processor and pulse to form a paste. Mix the blitzed figs with the toasted almonds and hazelnuts, sesame seeds, cloves and cinnamon. 3 Add the honey and 2 tablespoons of sherry to the fig mixture. Knead until smooth and the ingredients are incorporated. Add a splash more sherry if needed. Press the fig mixture into the lined tin and cover with the overhang of leaves or paper. Bake for 30 minutes, until the cover is a little crisp on top. Allow the wheel to cool, then wrap it in wax paper and tie with a pretty bow. This should keep for up to 2 weeks. **Note** Fig leaves in brine are available from specialist Mediterranean or Middle Eastern delicatessens.

HAZELNUT PRALINE BUTTER

EASY TOMATO CHUTNEY

HAZELNUT PRALINE BUTTER

This is fantastic melted over hot pancakes, spread on toast and with roasted or grilled fruit.

Makes 500g

- 250g hazelnuts
- 200g golden caster sugar
- 250g butter (room temperature), cut into large cubes

1 Preheat the oven to 200C/gas 6 and lightly oil a baking sheet. Pop the nuts onto the baking sheet and place in the oven for 4–5 minutes, till lightly toasted.
2 Combine the sugar with 6 tablespoons of water in a saucepan and bring to the boil till the sugar dissolves and starts to turn golden. Gently shake the pan from time to time so the sugar caramelises evenly, but try not to stir. When it's golden brown, turn it down to a simmer and add the nuts to coat in the caramel. Pour onto parchment paper to cool.
3 Blitz in a food processor until quite fine, then pulse in the butter. Spoon the praline butter onto a long sheet of greaseproof paper, roll into a log shape and refrigerate until needed. Serve on pancakes, grilled fruit or spread on toast.

HERB PESTO

Serves 2

- ½ garlic clove
- 2 handfuls of mixed herbs such as mint, parsley or tarragon
- 75g parmesan
- 75g pine nuts, toasted
- Extra-virgin olive oil

1 In a pestle and mortar, pound the garlic with a pinch of salt and pepper. Add the herbs and bash to a paste. Grate in the parmesan, add the pine nuts. Bash again then drizzle in the extra-virgin olive oil to loosen.

EASY TOMATO CHUTNEY

Makes 1 large jar

- 250g red onions, finely sliced
- 500g mixed tomatoes, roughly chopped
- 1 red chilli, deseeded, sliced
- 75ml red wine vinegar
- 140g brown sugar

1 Put everything in a pan over medium heat. Season to taste and stir well to combine. Simmer for 30–40 minutes or until jammy. Pour into a sterilised jar and leave to cool. Keeps for up to 4 weeks in the fridge. Perfect on toast with a chunk of mature cheddar.

ONION GRAVY

Serves 4-6

- 4 onions, very finely sliced
- A small knob of butter
- Olive oil
- 250ml white wine
- 2 sprigs of sage, leaves picked and finely sliced
- 300ml chicken or vegetable stock

1 Gently fry the onions in the butter and a splash of olive oil and cook slowly for about 40 minutes, until they're sticky and dark golden. Add the wine and reduce by half, then add the sage and stock. Season to taste. Bring to the boil before pouring over bangers and mash.

ANCHOVY BUTTER

Serves 4-6

- 1 garlic clove, chopped
- 4 anchovy fillets, chopped
- 1 tbsp chopped parsley
- ½ tbsp olive oil
- 150g butter

1 Pound the garlic, anchovy fillets, parsley, olive oil and a pinch of salt in a mortar until blended. Add the butter and pound again. Roll the butter in clingfilm to make a cylinder. Chill. To serve, remove the clingfilm, slice thinly and melt onto grilled steak.

MINT & PISTACHIO SAUCE

deglaze with a splash of vinegar, scraping up all the flavours left from cooking. Stir in the honey and mustard and bubble till it starts to thicken. If it looks too thick, add a splash of water or stock. Pop the meat back into the pan to coat in the sauce. Place the meat on plates, then pour over remaining sauce.

MINT & PISTACHIO SAUCE

Gloriously green, this is the perfect marriage of British Sunday lunch and delicate Middle Eastern fragrance.
Serves 8

- A large bunch of mint, leaves picked and roughly chopped
- A large handful of pistachios, bashed up
- 1–2 tbsp red wine vinegar
- 1½ tbsp rosewater
- 1 tsp honey

1 Combine the mint and pistachios, then add the other ingredients gradually. Taste and correct the seasoning, balancing the fragrant rosewater with the sharp vinegar and the sweet honey as you like. Serve with roast lamb.

RED WINE SAUCE

Team this easy classic with steak and mash for cold-weather comfort food.
Serves 4–6

- 1 garlic clove, finely sliced
- 1 bay leaf
- A few sprigs of rosemary, leaves picked and chopped
- 250ml red wine
- 1 vine of cherry tomatoes
- A good splash of chicken stock or water

1 Once you've fried your steaks, remove them from the pan and leave to rest. Now, add the garlic and herbs to the pan. Once the garlic is slightly coloured, pour in the wine and let it bubble for a couple of minutes. Add the tomatoes, squashing some with a fork so the juices mix together. If it looks too thick, add a splash of water or stock. Season to taste, spoon over your steaks and serve.

SALSA VERDE

This sauce brings a taste of spring to fish, pork and vegetable dishes.
Serves 4–6

- A handful each of parsley, basil and mint
- 1 garlic clove
- A small handful of capers
- 1 tbsp dijon mustard
- Juice of 1 lemon
- Extra-virgin olive oil

1 Put all the ingredients except the olive oil into a food processor and blitz until very finely chopped. Stir in enough oil to loosen to a spoonable consistency, then season with salt and pepper.

ROCKET PESTO

Serves 6 with pasta

- 150g rocket, roughly chopped
- 75g pine nuts, toasted and roughly chopped
- 2 garlic cloves, roughly chopped
- 50–75g parmesan, grated
- Extra-virgin olive oil

1 In a pestle and mortar, bash the rocket, pine nuts and garlic to a rough paste. Mix in the cheese. Add the oil to the desired consistency and season. Chill, covered with a layer of oil, in a sterilised jar for up to a week. Stir through cooked pasta.

HONEY & MUSTARD SAUCE

Make this to complement pan-fried chicken breast or pork chops.
Serves 4–6

- A good splash of white wine vinegar
- 4 tbsp runny honey
- 3 tbsp wholegrain mustard
- A good splash of chicken stock or water

1 Once you've pan-fried your meat, put the pan back on a medium heat and

HERBY LEMON SALT

- Lemon zest
- Fennel seeds
- Thyme
- Sea salt

1 For an exciting seasoning, pound lemon zest, fennel seeds and thyme with sea salt, all to taste. Using this mixture means you'll add less salt when seasoning food – you won't miss it with those other wonderful flavours.

....

PORK & CHESTNUT STUFFING

Making your own minced pork really turns your stuffing into something special. Usually you'd sweat the onions first, but this is one of those recipes that is quick and easy.

Makes enough to serve with 1 turkey

- 2 large onions, quartered
- 1kg pork shoulder, trimmed and diced
- About 50g stale bread
- 200g vac-packed chestnuts
- A bunch of sage, leaves picked
- 3 rashers smoked streaky bacon, roughly chopped
- White pepper
- 1 whole nutmeg, for grating
- 1 lemon
- 1 orange or clementine

1 Preheat your oven to 190C/gas 5. Blitz the onions in a food processor until finely chopped, then tip into the bowl with the pork. Tear the stale bread into small chunks and whizz into breadcrumbs. Add these to a large bowl, then crush and crumble your chestnuts in there too. Tip your diced pork mixture into the food processor with the sage leaves, bacon, a level teaspoon of freshly ground white pepper and a good pinch of salt. Finely grate in a quarter of the nutmeg, the zest of ½ lemon and just 2–3 gratings of citrus zest. Pulse until you've got some chunks and some mush, it won't even take a minute, then tip into the large mixing bowl with the bread and chestnuts. You really need to season this well, so add another pinch

HERBY LEMON SALT

of salt and white pepper, then scrunch it all up until well combined. If you want to test the seasoning before you stuff your bird, fry a tiny bit to check how it tastes when it's cooked, then adjust remaining mix to taste.

2 Take just under half of the stuffing out of the bowl to use for your turkey, then transfer the rest to an ovenproof dish that you can serve from. Use your hands to break it up and push it about, then flatten it all down. Pop it in the oven to cook for 50–60 minutes, or until bubbling and crispy. If you're doing it as part of your Christmas lunch, you want to get it on about the same time as your potatoes. When done, you can pour away any excess fat before serving if you want to. It will be soft, juicy and succulent on the inside, then crispy and chewy on the outside. Delicious. This is good the next day in all sorts of things – bubble and squeak, as part of a fry-up, in a leftover turkey sandwich.

SKORDALIA

This potent garlic sauce hails from Greece, where you'll find it served alongside fried vegetables, grilled meats and fried seafood, such as calamari. If you like, you could also substitute mashed potato or walnuts for the white bread.

Serves 2

- 3 slices of crustless white bread
- 5 garlic cloves
- 1 tsp sea salt
- 2 tbsp red wine vinegar
- A pinch of black pepper
- 6 tbsp olive oil

1 Soak the bread in bowl of water for 15 minutes, then squeeze out excess water. Crush the garlic cloves and sea salt in a pestle and mortar to make a paste. Transfer to a food processor, add the bread, red wine vinegar and black pepper. Slowly add the olive oil, blending until smooth and glossy.

LEMON PICKLE

1 Start by sterilising a 500ml jar. Put the feta into the jar, layering with lemon zest, thyme, a little salt and a pinch of pepper. Top up with olive oil to cover, then seal the jar. This will keep for up to 2 months unopened; once open, refrigerate and use within 2 weeks.

SPICED OLIVES
Makes a 500ml jar
- 1 tbsp coriander seeds
- Juice of ½ lemon
- 320g mixed black and green olives
- 1 dried red chilli
- 2 bay leaves
- About 250ml extra-virgin olive oil

1 Start by sterilising a 500ml jar. Split and slightly crush the coriander seeds in a pestle and mortar. Add them to the jar, along with the lemon juice, olives, chilli and bay leaves. Season with a little sea salt and a good pinch of pepper. Top up with olive oil to cover, then seal the jar. The olives will keep for up to 2 months unopened; once open, refrigerate and use within 2 weeks.

STICKY WHISKY GLAZE
Serves 2
- 2 tbsp honey
- 75ml whisky
- 1 crushed garlic clove
- 2 tbsp soy sauce
- Olive oil

1 Whisk the ingredients with salt and pepper. Place 2 steaks in a dish, cover with the marinade and chill for at least 2 hours. Barbecue or fry the steaks until sticky and done to your liking.

LEMON PICKLE
Makes 1 small jar
- 2 tbsp olive oil
- 1 tbsp yellow mustard seeds
- 1 tsp cumin seeds
- A small handful of curry leaves
- 2 unwaxed lemons, washed and finely chopped, pips discarded
- 3 tbsp caster sugar
- 1 small fresh red chilli, deseeded and finely sliced

1 Heat the oil in a small pan over a low heat and add the mustard and cumin seeds. When they start to pop, throw in the curry leaves. Fry for a minute or so, till they're nice and crisp. Add the lemons, sugar, chilli and a pinch of salt. Turn up to a medium heat and cook for around 10 minutes, or until thick, sticky and the lemons have softened. Leave to cool, then store in a sterilised jar in the fridge, where it will keep for up to a week. Serve with poppadoms.

SPICY PEPPER & CUCUMBER SALSA
- 1 red onion, finely chopped
- 1 pepper, deseeded and finely chopped
- 1 small cucumber, finely chopped
- 6 tbsp olive oil
- 3 tbsp vinegar
- 1 red chilli, finely chopped
- Juice of 1 lime

1 Combine the ingredients in a bowl. Season with salt and pepper and put aside to allow the flavours to mingle. Serve with grilled fish or chicken.

MARINATED FETA
This makes a delicious gift for a friend.
Makes 500ml jar
- 300g feta, cut into 2cm cubes
- Zest of 1 unwaxed lemon, peeled into thick strips with no pith
- 3-4 sprigs of thyme
- About 210ml extra-virgin olive oil

LEMONGRASS & MINT SUGAR

FANTASTIC FISH MASALA RUB

LEMONGRASS & MINT SUGAR

Makes 160g

- A bunch of mint, leaves picked
- 1 lemongrass stalk, halved lengthways and horizontally
- 150g golden caster sugar

1 In a pestle and mortar, bash the mint leaves to a green paste, then add the lemongrass and bash up. Add the sugar; bash again and mix well. Take out any large stalky pieces. Use this flavoured sugar to jazz up fruit salads or drinks.

FANTASTIC FISH MASALA RUB

Makes enough for 1 whole fish

- 1 tsp cardamom pods
- 1 tsp cumin seeds, toasted
- ½ tsp coriander seeds, toasted
- 1 dried red chilli
- 1 tsp black mustard seeds
- 12 curry leaves (optional)
- 1 tbsp garam masala

1 Crush the cardamom in a mortar and discard the shells, leaving the black seeds. Add the toasted coriander and cumin and bash till fine. Add the chilli, mustard seeds and curry leaves and pound. Add the garam masala and season. Rub fish with this before grilling.

CHRISTMAS BUTTER

This flavoured butter gives your turkey a sweetness and holds the skin away from the meat so it gets extra crisp. This is a job for Christmas Eve. It won't take long and will guarantee a delicious bird the day after. Another bonus is that the butter melting out will give you a self-basting bird.

Makes enough for 1 turkey

- 1 x 250g pack butter
- 75g dried cranberries, very finely chopped
- A few sprigs each of thyme, rosemary and sage, leaves picked
- Finely grated zest of 1 clementine

1 Put your butter into a bowl and add the cranberries. Chop all the herb leaves until fine, then add to the butter with the clementine zest and a pinch of salt and pepper. Mix until the butter softens and everything is combined. Divide the mixture roughly in half.
2 Get your turkey and use a spoon to work your way between the skin and the meat. Start at the side of the cavity just above the leg and work gently up towards the breastbone and towards the back so you create a large cavity. Push half your butter into the cavity you've created. Use your hands to push it through the skin right to the back so it coats the breast meat as evenly as possible. Do the same on the other side, then rub any leftover butter all over the outside of the bird to use it up. If you've got any herb stalks left over, put them into the cavity of the turkey for added flavour as it cooks. Cover the turkey in clingfilm and keep it in the fridge until you're ready to cook the next day.

MARINATED PEPPERS

Makes a 500ml jar

- 3 red peppers
- 4 garlic cloves, unpeeled
- 2 sprigs of rosemary
- 4 tbsp red wine vinegar
- About 150ml extra-virgin olive oil

1 Char your peppers over a direct flame on the hob or in a hot griddle pan until blackened and blistered. Pop in a bowl and cover with clingfilm for 5 minutes to steam off the skins.
2 Add the garlic cloves to the jar along with the rosemary sprigs, the vinegar and a good pinch of salt and pepper. When the peppers are cool enough to handle, peel off the skin, deseed and slice into 4cm-wide strips. Add to the jar and gently mix to combine. Top up with extra-virgin olive oil to cover, then seal the jar. The peppers will keep for up to 2 months unopened; once open, refrigerate and use within 2 weeks.

Yearbook index

Editor
Andy Harris
andy.harris@jamieoliver.com

Managing editor
Paul Dring
paul.dring@jamieoliver.com

Art director
Adrienne Pitts
adrienne.pitts@jamieoliver.com

Deputy editor
Holly O'Neill
holly.oneill@jamieoliver.com

Editorial assistant
Georgia Levy
georgia.levy@jamieoliver.com

Promotions & circulation manager
Julia Hall
julia.hall@jamieoliver.com

Editor-at-large
Jamie Oliver

Recipes
Paul Dring, Abi Fawcett, Laura Fyfe, Kevin Gould, Andy Harris, Anna Jones, Kate McCullough, Christina McCloskey, Jamie Oliver, Ginny Rolfe, Georgie Socratous, Sarah Tildesley

Photography & illustration
Steve Baxter, Laura Edwards, Tara Fisher, Jonathan Gregson, Dan Jones, David Loftus, William Meppem, Myles New, Britta Stenhouse, Sam Stowell, Yuki Sugiura

Advertising
Mark Rice and Ruth White, tel 020 7395 6000
mark.rice@touchdown-marketing.com
ruth.white@touchdown-marketing.com

Jamie Oliver Ltd
CEO John Jackson
Managing director Tara Donovan
Finance manager John Dewar

Subscriptions Jamie Magazine, 800 Guillat Avenue, Kent Science Park, Sittingbourne, Kent ME9 8GU 01795 414951, jamiemagazine@servicehelpline.co.uk

Australia, New Zealand, Canada and South Africa distribution: IPG, PO Box 393, Belmont, WA, Australia 6984; +61 8 9362 4134, wa@ipgonline.cc Newstrade distributor: NDD Pty Ltd, Building 5, 190-196 Bourke Rd, Alexandria, NSW, Australia 2015; +61 2 9381 3100

International distribution (excluding Australia, New Zealand, Canada and South Africa) by Seymour International Ltd, 2 East Poultry Avenue, London EC1A 9PT, +44 20 7429 1000

Jamie Magazine is published by Jamie Magazine Ltd. Registered Office 19–21 Nile Street, London N1 7LL, UK; 020 3375 5601.
Copyright 2010 Jamie Magazine Ltd. All rights reserved. Any reproduction without permission is prohibited. Jamie Magazine contains editorial content from external contributors, which does not necessarily reflect the views of Jamie Magazine Ltd. Jamie Magazine does not accept or respond to unsolicited manuscripts and photographs. The publishers do not accept responsibility for errors in advertisements or third-party offers. Jamie Magazine is printed by Artisan Press, Boston Road, Gorse Hill Industrial Estate, Leicester LE4 1AQ. ISSN 1759-0736 Print management & reprographic services by John Brown

Member of the Audit Bureau of Circulations

This magazine is printed on paper produced from sustainable managed forests accredited by the PEFC (Programme for the Endorsement of Forest Certification schemes; www.pefc.org).
PEFC/16-33-275

Useful information

Weight	
Imperial	**Metric**
1 oz	28g
1 lb	450g

Liquid	
1 teaspoon	5ml
1 dessertspoon	12ml
1 tablespoon	15ml
1 shot	25ml
1 small wineglass	125ml
1 large wineglass	250ml
1 fl oz	30ml
1 pint	568ml
1 glug	about 20ml

Cup measures		
	US	**AUS**
1 cup sugar	200g	220g
1 cup flour	115g	125g
1 cup liquid	240ml	250ml

Oven temperatures		
Celsius	**Fahrenheit**	**Gas Mark**
110C	225F	¼
130C	250F	½
140C	275F	1
150C	300F	2
170C	325F	3
180C	350F	4
190C	375F	5
200C	400F	6
220C	425F	7
230C	450F	8

For fan-assisted ovens, reduce temperatures by 10-20C

Ingredients

- We use Freedom Foods certified, free-range or organic pork and chicken and their by-products, including large eggs with an average weight of 60g.
- Whenever possible, we look for sustainably managed fish, with an MSC or Freedom Foods mark.
- We use beef gelatine or vegetarian setting agents, such as agar agar, and adjust for liquid quantity used in recipe according to packet instructions.
- Unless specified otherwise, all herbs in recipes are fresh, we season with freshly ground black pepper and sea salt, vegetables and fruits are washed and trimmed, and vegetables such as onions, garlic, carrots and potatoes are peeled.
- We test all recipes with semi-skimmed milk and always bake with golden caster sugar and unsalted butter, unless otherwise indicated.

Cooking tips

- Our recipes are tested in conventional ovens, using oven thermometers. For fan ovens, you are advised to reduce the temperature by 10-20C.
- To skin tomatoes, use a knife to place a small cross at the base of them. Place in a bowl, then cover with boiling water. Soak for 60 seconds, then drain off the hot water, cover with cold water, then peel off the skins. This also works for peaches and shallots.
- To sterilise a jar, wash jar and lid (removing rubber seal); place in the oven at 100C/gas ¼ for 30 mins, until dry. Immerse the seal in a pan of boiling water and simmer for 10 mins before removing with tongs. If you're reusing jam jars, wash jars and lids, then heat in the low oven.
- We use mixing bowls made from non-reactive materials such as glass, ceramic or plastic to prevent acidic reactions from marinades.